Deadication

That is not a typo. This b⟨ people I have known. My parents Israel and Rose, Grand Father Reverend Harry Jacobson and Grandmother Emma Cohen, brother Alan Jacobson, brother-in-law Richard Roemer, Tante Leah Bortnick, Aunt Ruth, Aunt Miriam, friend Tim Olive, best friends sister Judy Lempert and their parents Dan and Ruth Lempert. Mother–in-law Lois Roemer Breckenridge and father-in-law Paul Breckenridge and unfortunately many others. You have had a part in shaping who I am today and have inspired me to enjoy today. I miss you, love you and I thank you.

Livication

This livication is a dedication to all the living people.

This book is dedicated to YOU. I'm sure you awoke this morning and thought, "Gee, I could really use a book that was dedicated to me today." Well, now you have one.

Enjoy!

David Jacobson

Humor Horizons Publishing

Tucson, AZ 85730

"7 ½ Habits to help you become more Humorous, Happier & Healthier," by David M. Jacobson.

ISBN 978-1543050981

LCCN 2019900671

TABLE OF CONTENTS

Deadication..1

Livication...1

Partial Acknowledgements...5

AATH Acknowledgements..6

Introduction...9

The Chapter Before Chapter One: Overview of the seven and a half habits...17

Chapter One: Habit One – Treat humor as a necessity not a luxury...19

Chapter Two: Habit Two - Use self-effacing humor................30

Chapter Three: Habit Three: Look for humorous situations or create them with your imagination.......................................40

Chapter Four: Habit Four – Use the power of humor to positively influence you and others...51

Chapter Five: Habit Five -- Use humor to improve your communication..63

Chapter Six: Habit six – Humorize with your humor spirit........74

Chapter Seven: Habit Seven – Act like the highly humorous person you've become or are becoming................................88

Chapter Seven Point Five: The Half Habit - Mastering Your Thoughts...100

Chapter Eight: Putting Habits Into Practice..........................110

Chapter Nine: Pay Attention...117

Chapter Ten: Spirit of Humor..130

The Chapter That's Not a Chapter...........................….......137

Backward...140

Appendix B: Resources and recommendations for further
information. (Formerly "Appendix A" However, it had to be
removed due to emergency surgery. The "Gallbladder" section
also had to go.)...…................141

Partial Acknowledgements

There are too many people to acknowledge in the Acknowledgements. When I got to page 762 of acknowledgements, I gave up. That's why this is a Partial Acknowledgments.

Let me acknowledge:

David Lempert, my best friend, best man at my wedding and hopefully the best man at my funeral, although I don't know if funerals have best men. He has been my friend since we first met in 1961.

Laurie, my wife. She has been a great help with this book, and her insights and comments have helped to shape it, even though odds are she'll never read it.

Shira, Samuel, Yosef and Joshua, my children. They are all highly humorous people. Thanks Joshua and Darianne for the final proof read.

I acknowledge my editor, Kelly Epperson Simmons, not only because you're supposed to thank your editor, but because she gave me some great suggestions before she even began to edit this work.

I would also like to acknowledge my AATH (Association for Applied and Therapeutic Humor) friends, all my friends with arthritis, and my Mad Men on Mountain friends including Mike, Carl, Fred, Gordo, Ricardo, Path finder, Al, Jeremy, Jeff, Kevin, Jim, Jimmy, John, Brett, Steve, Sol, Mr. Natural, Roberto and Rob, Ron, Dean, Dave, Sam and whoever I forgot. I apologize if your name wasn't mentioned.

I acknowledge you, the reader who reads partial acknowledgements, because most readers don't read the acknowledgements, let alone partial ones. Statistics show that if you are mentioned in a book, you are more prone to like it and give positive feedback. This is why I am mentioning you, the reader who reads partial acknowledgements. Please write your name here _____. Thank you.

AATH Acknowledgements

This Acknowledgment is dedicated to my AATH friends. Can an acknowledgement be a dedication also? The answer is yes. AATH (Association for Applied and Therapeutic Humor) has hundreds of members, but these are the ones I feel a special connection to: Dr. Lee Berk, Ronald Berk, Karyn Buxman, Ed Dunkelblau, Lenny Dave, Mary Kay and Don Morrison, Katherine Puckett, Deb Price, Diane Roosth, Lenny Ravich, Madan Kataria, Steve Wilson, Chip Lutz, Joyce Saltzman, Beth Usher, Paul McGhee, Paul Osincup, Rod Martin, Allen Klein, Linda MacNeal, Don Baird, Yakov Smirnoff, Steve Sultanoff, Nila Nielsen, Maia Aziz, Don and Alleen Nilsen, Drew Tarvin, Waleed Salameh, Kay Caskey, Dwayna Covey, Beth Slazak, Shirley Trout, Frank Chindamo, Debbie Derflinger, Olubunmi Diala, Kyle Edgell, Pragito Dove, Adrienne Edmondson, Harald Ellingsen, Brenda Elsagher, Cheryl Fell, Rev Susan Sparks, Louis Franzini, Deb Gaudin, Saranne Rothberg, Guy Giard, David Glickman, Roberta Gold, Barbara Grapstein, Merlette Roberts, Margarita Gurri, Heidi Hanna, Debra Joy Hart, Earl Henslin, David Jacobson, wait that's me, Kathy Keaton, Cynthia Keeler, Jennifer Keith, Sporty King, Jill Knox, Jacki Kwan, Mary Laskin, Kathy Laurenhue, Lois McElravy, Rev Paul Moore, Melissa Mork, John Morreall, Amy Oestreicher, Kathleen Passinisi, Amy Robbins, Bronwyn Roberts, Michael Rousell, Patricia Shea, Megan Werner, Patty Wooten, Laurie Young, and Kelly Epperson Simmons who without meeting through AATH, I would not have helping me edit this book.

I'll take it one step further and venture to guess that if I didn't belong to AATH, I probably would not have written this book. This list of AATH friends goes on and on. There are so many more I could name, but I had to leave some out so that at the next conference they can say, "Hey, David, why'd you leave my name out?"

So now you know there's another benefit of belonging to AATH -- being named in a book - and it's not even a stated benefit! These are not "Facebook" friends, these are real people I see face to face, unless we're standing back to back or ass to ass.

I had no idea how many AATH friends I had until I wrote this acknowledgement. Many of these people were my humor heroes growing up and now I have the honor of calling them friends.

One more thing: This book is not to be construed as medical advice. If it was intended to construe medical advice, it would have been written by someone who gives medical advice. It is not intended to be construed as anything. Construing books can be very risky, so I urge caution whenever construing things.

Humor helps you keep your life in balance.

Introduction

There's a line in "The Galaxy Song" from the Monty Python album, *The Meaning of Life,* that states "there's bugger all down here on Earth." That's the reason I wrote this book, because there's bugger all down here on Earth. Your sense of humor can help make the experience of living with bugger less stressful, easier to cope with, and more joyful.

Do you consider yourself humorous, happy and healthy already? This book can take you up a notch. Or two. This book is for you.

Do you watch in puzzlement while everyone else in the room is laughing and think that you just don't get it? Do you often think, "That was so funny, I wish I said that?" This book is for you.

Are you the funniest person you know? This book is for you too.

Are you a short Jewish arthritic Director of Behavioral Health with a balding head and failing health? This book is for you. And, well, you may have written this book.

Please sit down and relax. Get comfortable. Like I said, this book is for you so laugh when you think something you read is funny. If you happen to be on a plane right now, laugh out loud and say: "Wow, this book is great!" Show the person next to you the book cover while you nod enthusiastically.

Before we go any further, I need to get one thing straight. This may be a humorous book written by a Certified Humor Professional, but that does not mean this book is frivolous or without important content.

This is not a "funny" book, although it will have humorous moments. This is a "fun" book, full of substance and an underlying serious message. The importance of humor matters deeply to me. I kid and joke, but the topic is the most important thing to me.

What I want you to know:

HUMOR CAN CHANGE YOUR LIFE FOR THE BETTER.

HUMOR CAN GET YOU THROUGH THE MOST CATASTROPHIC EVENTS OF YOUR LIFE.

HUMOR CAN HELP YOU CHANGE THE WAY YOU THINK SO THAT YOU CAN CHANGE THE WAY YOU FEEL

A PERSON WHO CAN USE THEIR SENSE OF HUMOR TO HELP THEM COPE IS THE MOST RESILIENT PERSON ON THE PLANET.

We all can use a little more resiliency.

If you picked up this book with the intention of cachinnating, (laughing loudly) (I learned that word from my editor Kelly's newsletter), then you have the wrong book. This is not a joke book or a crack-you-up laughing book.

This book may make you smile and possibly even laugh, but that is not its intention. The intention is to share some really great information that can help your life. My previous book had some great reviews, but it also had a review that said something to the effect of "This book didn't make me crack up." You have been warned so please do not write such reviews. Groucho Marx said, "People say I don't take criticism very well, but I say what the hell do they know?" David Jacobson said: "I embrace criticism, unless it's about me."

We will have some fun and a few laughs, and we will talk about the real ways to improve your life with these seven and a half habits. If you crack up, consider it a free bonus gift.

I grew up in the 1960s and 70s. At that time when greeting friends, you didn't say "Hi, how are you?" You said, "How high are you?" (This is an example of a chiasmus, which basically means an inverted word order in phrase. If you get nothing else from this book at least you got a new Scrabble word).

Imagine if you discovered a secret that could transform your life from miserable to remarkable. What would you do? Would you use that secret? I did. My secret was to use my sense of humor to overcome any obstacles that I came across. The intentional use of humor and laughter can take a painful experience and transform it into a joyful experience. Humor transformed my life.

We're human beings, we all have problems, that's a part of life. The question is pain. The answer is humor. We want to alleviate our suffering and others' suffering. Humor is one tool that can help you do that.

At the age of twenty-two, I found myself in critical condition with rheumatic fever and a severe form of arthritis. Initially, for a brief time I used drugs, alcohol and cigarettes to cope. I lost a potential athletic career, lost my favorite physical hobbies, lost my self-confidence and self-esteem tied to my physical body, and I lost my wallet, but that's a different story.

I've lived with the chronic pain of severe arthritis ever since and still do. Did humor make a difference in my life? What do you think? You don't even know me, but I bet you have a good guess. I can't promise that humor can turn you into a strong, handsome, successful, intelligent, witty and modest person like myself, but I can promise that you will be better off for trying some of the habits in this book.

"When one door of happiness closes, another one opens; but often we look so long at the closed door that we do not see the one which has opened for us." Helen Keller's words are true for me. I looked at the closed door for a long time.

I was barely able to walk and lived in excruciating pain. Every step felt like I was walking on shattered glass with fishhooks stuck into the bottoms of my feet, tugging my ankles and knees. In my debilitated state, I had to move back home and live with my mother. The first few weeks at my mother's apartment was the most trying time in my life. I had gone from a strong athlete at the beginning of October 1980 to a 110-pound weakling a few weeks later. It was a great effort to even chew and swallow food. When you are in critical condition, eating can become an Olympian task. I didn't even have the strength to raise my body up in bed. I was weak as a new born puppy. It took weeks to become strong enough to get into a wheelchair.

Any normal twenty-two-year-old would dread moving back home after just obtaining their independence, and I had also lost my body and my dreams. I had left the USA as a 130-pound version of Arnold Schwarzenegger and returned to Rochester, NY, as a skeleton who looked like he was just was released from a concentration camp.

My mother, Rose, the sweetest person in our family, who loved unconditionally, was very helpful. She was overly helpful. Taking care of me became her mission. Cooking, cleaning, doing the laundry and yelling out to me (imagine Edith Bunker's voice), *"What do you want for dinner?* She would sprint to get the phone every time it rang, shouting *"Oh, don't get up David, I'll get it!"*

I knew she would do everything for me. What I really needed at that point was to gain as much independence as possible. I did not want to become permanently disabled, totally dependent on others. I came up with a plan to get back on my feet. My first step was literally a humorous one. My goal was to beat her to the phone. This was an almost impossible feat considering how fast she moved and how slowly I dragged my painful body.

It was a Sunday afternoon in December in 1980 when the life transforming moment happened. What I did that day forever changed the course of my future. I waited for that phone to ring. It finally did.

"Ring, ring." "Ring, ring."

Rose called out, "Don't get up! I'll get it!"

I said to my mother, "No, wait! I'll get it!" I kind of dragged myself like Igor the hunchback, on the knuckles of my right hand touching the floor, drooling, tongue out and hobbling towards the phone. She was so busy laughing that I was able to beat her to the telephone. At that moment, the spirit of humor was revealed to me.

I realized the thoughts in my head affected my mood, which in turn affected my perspective. Even with the terrible pain, I could still have fun. I could still laugh. I could smile at my own idiocies. I could have fun thoughts replace the fearful and depressing ones. I could have a quality of life.

That is what I want for you. No matter what you have going on in your life, you can improve the quality. Improving your humor, happiness, and health starts with these simple habits shared here in these pages.

If I had to sum up what I hope you walk away with from this book, it would be the message of the following poem I wrote during an arthritis flare up:

A Place for Pain

I open the door, pain walks in

filling my home with darkness and discontent

I open the door, love walks in

replenishing the bedroom,

I open the door, faith walks in

illuminating my living room

I open the door, hope walks in

filling the kitchen with wonderful smells

I open the door, joy walks in

I explain that she has the wrong address

she should be next door

She comes in anyway

joy, like pain

knows not of manners or proper protocol

I open the door, humor walks in

It fills the empty spaces

Pain is still here

but, it has little room.

All the positive emotions will reduce the power of pain and put it in its proper place. Of all these positive emotions, it is the power derived from a sense of humor that has been my anchor, to hold me fast throughout the chaotic storms of life. I know humor can do the same for you.

The Chapter Before Chapter One

Overview of the 7 ½ Habits

Habit One: Treat humor as a necessity, not a luxury. Make humor a priority in your life. Some of the side effects will include improved physical health, improved attitude and improved mental health.

Habit Two: Use self-effacing humor. Its power comes from letting others know that you know your weaknesses and are comfortable with them knowing that you know they know. A master of self-effacing humor is confident and likeable.

Habit Three: Look for humorous situations or create them with your imagination. To become more humorous, you can discover or create unique associations among ideas. Children do this naturally. As we age, we tend to abandon our fantasy worlds and live mostly in the realm of rationality. Fantasy enhances our "real" world. Adults who can retain their childhood fantasy skills live more humorously than the rest.

Habit Four: Use the power of humor to positively influence you and others.

There is a connection between the sense of humor and overall well-being. Your sense of humor may also help others to improve their own well-being. Human being and well-being are not synonymous, could be an oxymoron, but not necessarily.

Habit Five: Use humor to improve your communication. Humor is a great communication tool. Humor helps you to have fun which reduces anxiety and knocks down common roadblocks that impede communication.

Habit Six: Humorize. By combining humor with all other aspects of life, your entire outlook will change. When you can take all parts of yourself and add the spirit of humor, you experience wholeness in a way that can't be described, only felt.

Habit Seven: Act like a humorous person. If it walks like a duck and quacks like a duck, it's a duck. Or someone who wants to be a duck. Act like the humorous, happy, healthy person you are or are becoming. With this attitude, you'll be able to reinforce and strengthen the other habits.

The Half Habit: Mastering your thoughts. This is a half habit because you don't need the whole habit for it to be effective. Yet it is the most difficult habit to maintain. Mastering your thoughts is a constant struggle; if you master them half the time, you'll be doing twice as well!

Choices: Upon your 90th birthday, please choose one of the following statements that best fits your life.

Choice One: "In my life, I spent more time worrying about things that might have happened, but didn't, or those that happened, but I couldn't change."

Choice Two: "In my life, I spent more time by using sense of humor than thinking negative worrying thoughts."

"No Humor, No Health. Know Humor, Know Health."

Chapter One:
Habit One – Treat humor as a necessity not a luxury.

We all need to eat, sleep and use the bathroom. These are the bare necessities of life. If you drank a gallon of prune juice an hour ago, you wouldn't say, "Ah, maybe I'll use the bathroom sometime" – no, you'd run to it now! Treat humor that importantly and your sense of humor – and your life - will greatly improve.

When I was a young child, my grandparents on my father's side died. I was too young to really mourn their loss, but not too young to forget the mirrors covered for the week of Shiva that our family observed. Shiva is the mourning period that Jewish families observe after the death of their relative. A couple years later when I was eight years old, I woke up on a Sunday morning and went into the bathroom and there was a sheet over the mirror. I knew someone else had died.

I went downstairs to watch cartoons. My mother came in and shut the TV off and told me I couldn't watch TV. When I asked why, she told me that my father had died.

I ran up to my room and sat numbly on my bed in a state of shock. My best friend David came over and my mother told him it was okay for him to go up to my room. We just sat there together for what may have been hours. I don't know how he had the wisdom to do that, to just sit quietly with me, but he did, and it was just what I needed at the time.

In the movie *Good Will Hunting*, Robin Williams said: "You don't know about real loss because it only occurs when you've loved something more than you love yourself." At the age of eight, I learned about real loss.

When I returned to school after the mourning period, all my classmates had made condolence cards for me. My family and I read them that evening in our dining room. One of cards said: "I'm sorry your father died. I would be sad too if my fat father had died," with the word fat crossed out. We all laughed heartily. It was the first laugh we had since the day my father died and it helped. That is when I really understood that humor is a necessity, a real part of life, not some kind of luxury.

When I returned to school, I was somewhat of a behavioral problem, bouncing off the walls, not able to sit still for more than ten minutes. Today they call it ADHD, then it was called a behavioral problem. I failed the third grade that year, not because of my school work but because of my "behaviors." I was "too immature" to go on to the next grade.

The next year, one of the common punishments for bad behavior was to sit in the closet where our winter coats were hung. These closets had sliding doors that could be pulled down. When the teacher was distracted, I slowly pulled the closet door down. In the dark, I climbed up into my winter coat that was on the hook and slipped into the arms. The problem was the coat was still on the hook and I couldn't get out, I was just hanging in the coat on the hook.

The teacher opened the closet and the whole class saw me dangling in my coat on the hook, so I just started waving my arms around at them while hanging and the class and the teacher cracked up. My first stand up, or hooked up, routine and I loved the attention and the laugher. I found my role and place in the classroom as a child humorist, a term I think is much better than class clown.

Without my father around, our home was filled with violence as my older siblings fought each other and fought with me, or rather beat on me. The local emergency room was very familiar with our family. As the traumas grew so did my need to use humor as a coping mechanism. Humor became an absolute necessity.

On a first date is humor a luxury or necessity? If you want a second date, humor better be part of that first date. We need to smile and laugh and see humor every day, every chance we get, every single day.

There are times not to laugh - not many though - like when telling someone bad news or when someone is changing a flat tire, but other than that, there's usually a health benefit to laughter.

Laughter makes us feel better, in mind, body, and spirit.

My life experience, personally and professionally, has proven that to me over and over. I am not a professional comedian, I am a humorist. What is the difference between a humorist and a comedian? A comedian tells jokes to make people laugh. A humorist makes a point with humor. We look for the humor in natural situations that people take for granted most of the time. Think Mark Twain, Dave Barry or David Sedaris. They show us how humor is a necessary part of everyday life.

Three of my favorites from these fellas:

Mark Twain: Be careful about reading health books. You may die of a misprint.

Dave Barry: It is a well-documented fact that guys will not ask for directions. This is a biological thing. This is why it takes several million sperm cells to locate a female egg, even though the egg is, relative to them, the size of Wisconsin.

David Sedaris: I always think it's a good policy to like the people who like you.

Humorists typically won't make you crack up hard enough to wet your pants. We can get a point across in a humorous fashion that will improve your chances of retaining the information because you learned this new information in a fun way.

It is common knowledge now that those who incorporate humor into educational material will have that material remembered longer than those that offer educational material in a drab, stuffy, cold or monotone way. We all remember the teachers we had that used humor. We appreciate doctors or co-workers or bosses that use humor. You can learn to use humor too.

This first habit advises you to acknowledge the importance of appreciating humor. It's not how many jokes you can tell, or even how many you hear. It's how much you can appreciate the humor that surrounds you in your everyday life.

As human beings, we are responsible for our own lives. Be someone who has the strength to accept things they can't change and change the things they can, for example, your underwear.

A person with a poorly developed sense of humor is a person who is driven by feelings, circumstances, conditions, and the environment. They are tossed like a boat in stormy water without oars. A healthy happy humorous person is guided by his or her own purpose in life, with a clear mind, tempered with humor. A person with humor takes the bull by the horns and hangs Christmas ornaments on them, or if they're Jewish they hang Hanukah candles on them.

Make humor as necessary as brushing your teeth. You can practice in daily situations. Say for example, someone makes a snide remark about your weight: "When are you planning to go on a diet?"

Reaction without humor: "You son of a…" (You're so mad you pick up a refrigerator and throw it at the person.)

Reaction with humor: "When I start a new weigh of life!"

Or you get another snide remark from some young whippersnapper: "You Boomers think you are so special. Get over the sixties already and join the 21st century."

Reaction without humor: The blood rushes to your head, you pop a vein in your temple and have a stroke. You spend the rest of your life drooling and can only enjoy such novels as *Fun with Dick and Jane* and *My Dog Spot.*

Reaction with humor: "Oh Yeah." or "Youth cannot know how age thinks and feels. But the old are guilty if they forget what it is to be young." Or just smile and walk away. Or drive away on your scooter.

Maybe you get pulled over for a speeding ticket. When you roll down your window the officer says, "I've been waiting for you all day."

Reaction without humor: "The driver you just let go by was driving at least 10 miles faster than me! If you did your job right, you would have pulled over the right guy!" The officer orders you out of the car, tells you he suspects you're hiding drugs and does a cavity search before he hauls you off to jail.

Reaction with humor: "Yeah, well I got here as fast as I could." The cop laughs and sends you on your way without a ticket.

We can't control the events that occur in our life, but we can control our responses to those events. If you haven't heard this a hundred times already, you haven't heard enough motivational speakers or read enough self-help books. When conflicts and problems occur, they are usually the result of one of three situational areas: Our actions (the behavioral results of our attitude and underlying beliefs); the actions of others (the behavior of others, which results from their attitudes and underlying beliefs); our memories of past actions or thoughts about future actions and situations.

Those that treat their humor as a necessary and important component of their life evaluate their own behavior, find the humor in their actions, and laugh at it. As Paul Riser said, "Use humor to confront problems not avoid them."

The impulse for revenge or other petty useless actions dissolves. Humor brings wisdom to some, joy to others, and smiles of amusement to just about everyone else.

Victor Frankl, a psychologist in the Freudian tradition, recognized that "between stimulus and response, man has the freedom to choose." The capacity human beings have of taking an objective stance towards their own life, or stepping outside themselves, is the basis, Frankl tells us, for humor. And, as he noted in the concentration camps, "Humor was another of the soul's weapons in the fight for self-preservation." Humor was a necessity, not a luxury.

We can't control the behavior of others, but we can control our response. Situations and circumstances are always there. Life happens. How you deal with it is what matters. That is when humor is our necessity.

Several years ago, I was invited to give a guest sermon at a Universalist Unitarian Church on the subject of "humor and spirituality." The church was on the other side of the city and I was running late. Stressed out in traffic and watching the time, a guy cut in my lane right in front of me and his back bumper barely missed my front bumper by 1/16th of an inch, or two atoms and one electron. We were heading for the stop light and I was pissed off! I couldn't wait to pull up next to him, so I could give him "the look." The equivalent of giving the finger, except with a facial expression instead.

As I approached the stop light, I thought about where I was going and for what purpose. I decided a different tactic would be more in line with my sermon and my purpose in life. When we reached the light, I put my disabled placard on the mirror, pulled my arms out of my sleeves and tucked them in my shirt and bit the steering wheel with my teeth! The guy turned to see me, the person he just cut off. His eyes grew wide as he looked over and saw a man with no arms, biting the steering wheel with his teeth.

I slightly turned towards him, grinned at him with my teeth still holding the steering wheel and nodded my head. He had a shocked look on his face and appeared to feel awful for cutting off the poor pathetic armless guy. I wasn't mad anymore and he wasn't either. Because humor was a necessity rather than a luxury at that moment, a potentially explosive situation turned into a milder humorous situation that was totally non-threatening.

Humor not only helps transform your mood and the moods of others, it helps you make connections with others. Connections are the most valuable gift we as human being offer each other. Much of humor is born from suffering and pain, but that pain and suffering helps enhance your humor abilities to the point of enlightenment through humor.

There is nothing I appreciate more than my friendships and interactions with others. It is because of humor that many of these interactions were initiated. Humor humanizes you and makes you approachable and open to new relationships that can and most likely will enrich your life. I find this to be one of the absurdities of life that out of pain comes the ability to connect with others, and out of those relationships comes comfort, connection, contentment (and many other words that begin with C).

When you can realize that humor is not an "extra" something to add to your life, but an inherent daily component, you will start to lighten up internally. Feeling lighter feels good.

This first habit is easy. Humor is free. Take as much as you want. There is enough for everyone.

Regarding my story above, I offer an apology to those with no arms: If you have no arms and were offended by my story, I am sorry, and don't have a leg to stand on. Please forgive me. If you don't have a leg to stand on and were offended by the above statement, I am sorry about that too. If you don't have teeth and can't bite the steering wheel, then I guess I'm sorry about that too.

Treating humor as necessity, not as a luxury, means treating your humor like a musician would treat their instrument, their most valued possession. It is something you possess, so take good care of it. Nurture it and watch it grow.

Chapter Two:
Habit Two - Use self-effacing humor

Know your weaknesses and turn them into strengths. (Begin with your rear end in mind.)

My wife came home after her complete physical when she turned fifty. She stood in front of the mirror in her underwear admiring herself. I came home not in the best mood and asked her, "What are you doing?"

She said, "Dr. White said I should be very proud at the shape I'm in. I have four children yet have the physiology of a twenty-year-old."

"Did she mention your fifty-year-old ass?" I asked.

Laurie gave me a look, thought for a second and responded "No, your name didn't come up at all."

Okay, Laurie will tell you that this story isn't true, but I love this story. It is the epitome of taking a potentially volatile situation and defusing the conflict with humor.

Another piece of advice: Be comfortable with your ass. I do not take my ass seriously, and neither should you. I mean you shouldn't take yours seriously either. Chances are you may never have even seen my ass so it would be difficult for you to take it seriously anyway. The more you look at your ass, the more you should be able to realize that it doesn't change based on how often you look at it or feel about its current shape. If it currently looks great, that's super! Just keep in mind that eventually if you live long enough it will turn into jiggly gelatin. Well, most likely. And always, always, be kind to the ass of your significant other.

According to my friend and fellow AATH colleague, psychologist Rod Martin, there are four styles of humor: affiliative, self-enhancing, aggressive, and self-defeating humor. Affiliative and self-enhancing are adaptive styles. They are beneficial to your well-being. Aggressive and self-defeating are maladaptive. They obviously are detrimental to your well-being.

This book is about improving your well-being. When I say self-effacing, it is self-enhancing humor. This is having the ability to laugh at yourself, such as making a joke when something bad or embarrassing has happened to you.

What I think I look like   What I actually look like

When someone notices I'm limping, I let them know I have arthritis and am having a small flare up. When they respond with "Oh, I didn't know you have arthritis" or "Gee, you're too young to have arthritis" (I used to hear that a lot in my twenties, not so much in my sixties), I respond with a light comment such as "Yeah, I won the wrong lottery." That is self-effacing humor. Perhaps you trip over the curb and someone gives you a look. You can smile and say, "I have two left feet even though I'm right handed."

These comments state that it's okay, I can laugh at this and you don't need to feel uncomfortable about it. This is the safest type of humor to use with those you may not know that well. It is difficult to be offended by someone who is simply poking fun at himself. It is important to clarify that poking fun at yourself is not the same as putting yourself down.

Self-effacing humor can be either self-enhancing or self-defeating depending on how it is used. Healthy humor is NOT self-defeating. Do not use self-defeating humor, it only serves to reinforce negative thoughts and is very unhealthy for those with fragile self-esteem or problems with self-confidence.

For those prone to depression, self-defeating humor can be detrimental. Aggressive and self-defeating humor leads to lower levels of happiness and are associated with anxiety, depression, hostility, and aggression. Self-effacing humor that is self-enhancing boosts your self-esteem and high levels of self-esteem leads to happier and healthier lives.

A Humor Style Quiz, created by my pal Rod, can help you find out what type of style you identify with the most. You can find a link to that quiz in the Appendix. Or maybe it's the Gall Bladder.

Affiliative and self-enhancing humor are linked to extraversion and openness to new experiences. That gets you on the path to being more humorous, happier, and healthier. Self-effacing humor used the right way is self-appreciating humor. You recognize the absurdities you encounter in life and make a conscious decision to laugh at the cosmic joke of life instead of crying about it. Like Billy Crystal said, "I don't like heights. This is why I stopped growing at fifth grade."

You do not necessarily have to make fun of yourself with self-effacing humor if that's too close for comfort. You can generalize about your family, your neighborhood, or any other group you are affiliated with. Historically, jesters in medieval courts would make fun of themselves to amuse kings and queens.

When you can find the humor in everyday situations and make yourself the target of the humor in a good-natured way, this is a healthy way of coping with stress. Laughing at yourself is the highest and healthiest form of humor. Using self-effacing humor is the safest way to introduce humor to those you don't know that well. It helps build rapport and trust. Poke a little fun at yourself to open some communication.

I come from Rochester, New York, where having a nasal twang is normal. People from other parts of the country can tell I have a distinct accent. Many of "my people" who also speak like me are unaware of the "accent." People that use self-effacing humor are more aware of these quirks and can be playful. No one gets defensive and we all have a little fun.

My version of self-effacing humor? I'm a short, overweight, balding, Jewish, arthritic man. I can laugh, or I can cry about that. I choose to laugh. Why can I poke fun at what I am today? A big stomached thin-armed late middle age man? The memories of myself as that Olympian-built David of yesteryear. That will sustain me the rest of my life and I am thankful for those memories.

It comes down to what is important. My ego? My memory? Or my relationships? Clearly relationships are what drive me forward. I'm excited to meet and learn from new people, including young people, Gen X, Millennials and Z and even baby boomers like myself. It never ends, we learn until the day we die. The day we stop wanting to learn is the day we begin to die. Humor helps us break the ice in all situations.

Self-effacing / self-enhancing humor works well because it's safe and does not lead to a loss of respect. If you have a "superior" vocational position such as a CEO, CFO, CMO, OREO, or any other C with an O, humor indicates that you are human and approachable. Self-effacing humor gets its strength from playing with your weaknesses. People that have the ability to laugh at themselves in just the right measure are perceived as secure, confident, strong, attractive and likeable.

Poking fun at yourself gives the message that "Hey, look at my ass, do you see any stick up it? No, I don't have a stick up my ass. I am not uptight. I walk with a smooth cool sway of a humorous person." Or something like that. (I think my mom (and my editor) will tell me I am using the word ass too much. Sorry. I'll stop now.)

I'm confident in my use of self-effacing humor. I come from a place of confidence. I know I am a humorous person and that feels good. Humor gives me that feeling of strength that we all need to sustain us, but don't acknowledge in public that it is needed. I accept who I am. I don't envy people. There's not enough time for envy or greed, or other negative thoughts. Life is short and I want to enjoy the ride. Humor helps power the ride.

Rodney Dangerfield is a great example of self-effacing humor. By self-report he says he was ugly, stupid and fat. We know that's not true, but his approach made him relatable. He left us with many great zingers, like this one: "My father gave me a bat for Christmas, first time I tried to play with it, it flew away."

Another one-liner that comes from Rodney, "It takes a lot of balls to golf the way I do." Many comedians use this style of humor. Phyllis Diller said, "You know you're old when someone compliments you on your alligator shoes and you're barefoot." As a Jewish man, I can make the old joke, "Circumcision is popular because Jewish girls won't touch anything that's not at least 15% off."

Self-effacing humor gives others the message that I'm a human being just like you. I'm a human doing - doing things just like you. I'm a human saying, talking just like you. I'm a human listening - listening half-heartedly just like you.

Look for opportunities to see your humorous side and poke fun at it. This will be one of your most powerful tools to connect with others and a subtle way to show your strength.

Groucho and Chico of the Marx Brothers fame were both funny and very different in their lifestyles. Groucho was conservative financially, investing in blue-chip stocks. Chico was a gambler and often lost and regained his fortune. He relied on his older brother to bail him out.

The reckless Chico was often lectured by Groucho on planning for the future and investing wisely. When Groucho bailed Chico out, Groucho always asked him what shape the world was in. Chico would respond, "Better with a brother like you in it."

When the stock market crashed, Groucho lost everything. He now needed his brother to bail him out. When Chico helped out Groucho, he asked, "What's the shape of the world? Groucho responded, "Better with a brother like you in it."

My brother Alan did make the world better for me. He was a humorous person and my world was a better because he was in it. My oldest brother died before I got to show him this book. I miss him and his sense of humor. I'm glad I have all the memories of laughing with him, it helps me get through the grieving times. He lived his life to the fullest and though I miss him, I'm glad he lived his life on his own terms. Humor was a large part of our bonding.

Humor helps us bond with everyone. Humor, including self-effacing humor, is a great characteristic of a leader. Leadership is taking the risk of saying the things that make others laugh or smile to drive your point home. If those that admire you follow suit, you have more than doubled your effect on the world. Abe Lincoln was a master of self-effacing humor. He viewed humor as a necessity to deal with his seemingly insurmountable troubles.

One of Lincoln's most famous quotes comes from addressing his cabinet with the following: "Gentlemen, why don't you laugh? With the fearful strain that is upon me night and day, if I did not laugh occasionally I should die, and you need this medicine as much as I do."

Lincoln was a master storyteller. Often, he focused on his awkward gait, his being referred to as an uneducated rail-splitter and his not very photo-friendly face, using these characteristics to make himself the butt of his own jokes. His self-effacing humor was very disarming to anyone who came into conflict with him.

Lincoln often visited hospitals in the Washington area. He asked wounded soldiers about their health and entertained the patients with his stories. There is an unsubstantiated story that implies after one such visit, a journalist followed him to the same hospital and heard wounded soldiers laughing and talking about the president. The soldiers seemed in such good spirits that the journalist was curious, and overheard one soldier say that even though he lost a leg, he'd be glad to lose the other if he could hear more of the president's stories.

I might not literally give an arm or leg for humor, but I know its importance. I trust you are understanding that more and more. If not, shut this book. Open it up again at the first page and begin again.

Chapter Three:

Habit Three - Look for humorous situations or create them with your imagination.

While in Jerusalem, Israel, as I boarded the city bus one day, I noticed a Palestinian mom with her three young sons. She gave each of them some chocolate. The boy who looked about four years old immediately crammed his chocolate bar in his mouth. Then he glanced at his six-year-old brother, grabbed his chocolate bar right out of his hand and shoved it into his stuffed mouth. The shocked brother glared at him in disbelief, jumped up and down, yelling and shouting. The oldest brother fell to the ground cracking up laughing.

As the bus drove off, I too was laughing. I had enjoyed a humorous scene, because I had my eyes open for one. Always look for humorous situations. They are everywhere. Especially with kids. This scene could have easily been me and my brothers. Seeing the humor in this instance made me laugh and also took me back to a thousand memories of funny times. Humor has a way of compounding like that.

As you look for humorous situations, you will also see the universality of humor. I promise you, humor is everywhere if you are willing to look for it. Humor allows us to see that we all have more in common than differences.

Humor breaks down barriers and can be a tool for peace.

When I was in Israel, I had Palestinian friends and that was mostly due to the humor we shared, the laughs we had together. Humor didn't distinguish between Muslim and Jew. With humor there is no judgement. Humor creates connections with other people no matter what race, political party, religion, or status, or whether Trekkies or not.

Just like in Habit One where it's about how much you appreciate humor rather than how many jokes you tell, the same is true for searching for humor. The more you exercise your humor muscles, the stronger they'll get. The more you seek, the more you find.

Use your observations, and your imagination and fantasies, to create humorous situations. A great example of creating humorous situations with his mind is the James Thurber character, Walter Mitty. If you haven't read the short story or seen the movie, I highly recommend you do. I recommend anything written by James Thurber, he was a great American humorist.

It is important to use your sense of humor to develop it to a higher level. While working as a Trauma Social Worker, I made it my mission to find the humor anywhere I could. The hospital setting can be stressful, especially when you're telling loved ones that their spouse, mother, father, sister, brother, or child did not survive.

It was on a day like this when I was busy and stressed out that I got on the elevator and it was empty. This rarely happens during the hustle and bustle of the hospital. I was the only one in, so I celebrated! I jumped up and down and danced, singing out loud, "Hurray, the elevator's empty!"

When the doors opened, I had a big smile on my face, truly feeling the spirit of humor. When I walked into the next patient's room, I was glowing happy, not a phony smile but authentically happy.

Do you think this can impact a patient? Absolutely. Think about how many people walk into a patient's room. Usually, the visitor is a relative or a friend that feels sad their loved one is there. Or it's a staff member who needs to get something from them, like blood, a stool sample, or urine. Or it's a doctor with their entourage of students, intern's residents, lions and tigers and bears.

If you can walk into a room genuinely happy and share that mood with someone, it can help, in any situation, especially a hospital.

I recall walking into the room of a young man, "Jack" and he said, "It's good to see a smiling face."

I asked, "Why?"

Jack said, "Because I'm scared to death about this surgery today and you distracted me for a moment."

Jack was there for a serious heart operation and was told he may not survive. I asked what would make him less scared. He said, "To know right away I survived the surgery."

I thought for a second. "Tell you what, how about I put a big sign on the wall in Post Op so that when you wake up, the first thing you see is this sign that says YOU ARE HERE."

Jack said he'd like that.

He survived the surgery. (Do you think I would share this story if he had not?) Jack later shared with me that after the surgery he awoke groggy and looked at the wall. It oriented him to see the big YOU ARE HERE sign, and it made him smile. It may have been a silly little thing, but he told me that he would never forget that little piece of humanity waiting for him in Post-Op for as long as he lived.

Humor used in the hospital setting is usually the witty and playful type. Fun chitchat between staff and patients eases the embarrassment of losing any modesty. Staff members see patients at their most intimate times. Patients come into the hospital, are stripped of their clothes and put into a hospital gown with their butt hanging out. They are told when to eat, what to eat, when they can have visitors and when visitors must leave. It is not a day at the spa!

You may not see it, but there is more humor in a hospital setting than a comedy club! It's just a little subtler. Examples are endless.

A toddler walked up to me and threw her diaper at me, and I laughed and responded, "Oh, a gift for me! Thank you so much!" I walked into the room of a patient with severe cerebral palsy disease, and he said, "Need a milk shake, I can really stir!" Another patient passed gas quite loudly and told me his roommate is a ventriloquist.

A ninety-year-old patient asked me if I could provide him a female social worker with large breasts, so I came back two minutes later with cloth stuffed in my shirt and told him this is the best I could do. I walked into a room of a 75-year-old female cancer patient who immediately lifted her gown to show me the wound on her behind. I said, "I'm a social worker, not a doctor." She said, "Yeah, well, at my age, I rarely get to show my body to a young handsome man, so I'm going show it!"

If humor is needed anywhere, it's in a hospital. Maintaining levity, in any way we can, makes the stressful not so stressful. Humor is another way of letting patients know you care about them.

In the ICU, I've worked with hundreds of patients so remembering each one is not my gift. A former patient once came up to me at a mall. He said, "Hey David, remember me?" Non-recognition was evident on my face. He said "Okay," then pulled his head back as if he were looking directly up to the ceiling, put a finger in his mouth and pulled it as if it were a fishhook jerking and stretching his cheek. He began to make a gurgling sound. I said "Oh, yeah, you were in the ICU!"

You can look for humor absolutely everywhere. What amuses you? Do you know what types of humor are attractive to you and the styles you prefer? Find the stuff that YOU think is funny. There are all kinds of comedy, (and hence a variety of comedians/shows to watch and types of humor books to read.)

For example:

Observational Humor: Jerry Seinfeld says "Did you ever notice…"

Topical Humor: Jay Leno says "In the news today…"

Character Humor: Carol Burnett in any of her famous sketches.

Prop Humor: Carrot Top. Gallagher. My NSA colleague Tim Gard, and his rubber chicken hanging out of his suitcase.

Physical Humor: Jim Carrey, Jerry Lewis.

Impressionists: Kevin Pollack, Dana Carvey, and Mike Meyers.

Improvisation: Robin Williams, Paula Poundstone.

Humorous situations are all around us and everywhere in the world. They're in books, audiotapes, movies, TV shows and daily interactions. Some stand the test of time, and yet there is new fresh humor every day. All we have to do is look for it.

Be advised that when sharing humor, there is appropriate and inappropriate humor. The basic rule for identifying inappropriate and unhealthy humor is that it is exclusive, separates people, puts someone down, ridicules others, destroys self-esteem, uses stereotypes of groups, encourages a negative atmosphere, offends others or lacks awareness of others' feelings. In fact, research shows that laughing at inappropriate humor has no health benefits, whereas laughing at positive appropriate humor has numerous physiological, social and psychological benefits.

Appropriate humor is inclusive. It brings people together. It is shared with all. It decreases prejudice by focusing on the universal human experience. It encourages a positive atmosphere. It builds rapport and trust. It is based on caring and comes from a place of love. It is supportive and builds confidence. It can be self-effacing, like you read about in Habit Two, role modeling how to poke fun at oneself without being negative or too self-critical.

What should you do when someone uses inappropriate humor around you and you don't like it? There are several responses open to you depending on the type of person you are or mood that you are in.

1. The make-them-think approach: You can ask them to retell the same joke or story again using themselves or their group as the main character instead of the race, religion, nationality or sex they used in the joke or story. Most will say, "Then it's not funny." Sometimes the lightbulb will go off and they'll understand. Sometimes not, but at least you will have stood up for positive healthy humor.

2. The direct approach: You can simply state that you don't appreciate that kind of humor and ask they please not use it in front of you. A simple, friendly, "I don't find that kind of humor amusing" is enough to diffuse any more unhealthy jokes.

3. The indirect approach: Choose not to laugh or smile at the end of the joke. You may go as far as putting on an angry face if that's how you feel.

4. The educational approach: You could choose to educate them by explaining the differences outlined above between inclusive and exclusive humor. This will permit them a face-saving response. For example, you could say something like "I'm sure if you were aware of how mean-spirited that joke makes you sound you wouldn't use it."

Any of these responses could be done privately or in a group. The peer pressure of a group may have a stronger impact on the person and lets others know how you feel about offensive humor at the same time.

Most people offend others and tell poor jokes out of ignorance. We all have different tastes in humor like we do with food. What is offensive to some is funny to others.
In certain professions there is gallows humor and other types that the public would not understand, but really serve a healthy purpose as a coping mechanism in a stressful and dire workplace such as an emergency room.

Another exception is with your closest friends and family. Sometimes "inappropriate" humor is the funniest between immediate friends and family. When there is agreement that it isn't offensive to either party, then there's permission to use it. My friend Kevin and I share a lot of "arthritis" humor that others wouldn't find funny and some with arthritis may even be offended by, but for us, it's hysterical and healthy.

You can find the funny everywhere. And you can also use your imagination to inject humor. A childhood memory comes to my mind. At the age of five, I heard a knock at the front door of our house. My siblings told me to open the door.

I reached way up to the knob, turned it and opened the door. There standing one foot tall at the door was a gnome, with a red hat hood, blue tunic and blue pointed slippers. My brother said, "Wow, it's the King of the Elves. You have to name him."

"His name is Chuckles," I answered without hesitation. I believed Chuckles was alive. I had a very vivid imagination and swore I'd seen him move from the corner of my eye many times. He was magical, and I thought he had magical powers.

As a child no one ever heard me say, "I'm bored." My imagination kept me company wherever I went. I could sit for hours watching people, thinking "Hmm that guy is a spy working for an enemy government, he's waiting to meet his contact."

Your imagination can help you find humor. When driving through Texas, I saw the sign for the town of Marfa. Do you know about Marfa, TX? Well, an old oil tycoon billionaire generously helped his town. This man also had a speech impediment. The town wanted to honor him and told him he could name the town whatever he wanted. He immediately knew the name he wanted. "Let's call it Marfa after my wife."

The next day he had a heart attack and spent a week in the hospital. On his return home, he saw the Marfa signs everywhere. Everyone expected him to be happy, but he was not. His wife's name was Martha.

So I made the above story up. It's one of many examples of how imagination can help us create humor while on a road trip. Even when you are driving in the car alone, you can find humor. If life is a highway, humor gets us over the speed bumps.

When you are able to implement the humor habits, you find that you feel happier and when you feel happier, it has a positive impact on your stress level and that leads to a healthier you. Don't make life harder than it has to be! Find the humor!

Chapter Four:

Habit Four – Use the power of humor to positively influence you and others.

David & Dwayna Covey at AATH conference

Several comedians have had an influence on me.

Steven Wright: Right now, I'm having amnesia and deja vu at the same time. I think I've forgotten this before.

It's a small world, but I wouldn't want to have to paint it.

Robin Williams: Why do they call it rush hour when nothing moves?

Billy Crystal: In high school, I was the class comedian as opposed to the class clown. The difference is the class clown is the guy who drops his pants at the football game, the class comedian is the guy who talked him into it.

What's so fascinating and frustrating and great about life is that you're constantly starting over, all the time, and I love that.

Demetri Martin: The worst time to have a heart attack is when you're playing a game of charades.

Steve Allen: One of the nice things about problems is that a good many of them do not exist except in our imaginations.

Asthma doesn't seem to bother me any more unless I'm around cigars or dogs. The thing that would bother me most would be a dog smoking a cigar.

Groucho Marx: Outside of a dog, a book is man's best friend. Inside of a dog, it's too dark to read.

Like my acknowledgements, the list goes on and on.

Groucho also said: "I, not events, have the power to make me happy or unhappy today. I can choose which it shall be. Yesterday is dead, tomorrow hasn't arrived yet. I have just one day, today, and I'm going to be happy in it."

Groucho Marx was right, all we have is today. So we might as well laugh.

Never underestimate your influence on others or the world, and never underestimate the power of humor. Sharing your sense of humor with others can be very beneficial, both for you and them.

If you can use humor to engage and entertain others no matter what their political affiliation or beliefs or race or gender, you possess a valuable gift. Your humor will be appreciated. Humor has the ability to connect us. It has the power to heal.

Perhaps you've heard that the Old Testament references the healing properties of humor: "A merry heart doeth good like a medicine." Although our ancestors couldn't explain it scientifically, they knew intuitively that laughter was good for the body as well as the soul.

More recently than the Old Testament, Norman Cousins, in his book, *Anatomy of an Illness*, described how he used humor to help cure himself. Cousins watched old Marx Brother's movies, *Candid Camera*, and other funny shows and laughed uncontrollably. He believed his own laughter played a significant role in overcoming his disease.

What Norman said was true for me. When I cracked up laughing for even ten minutes, I could get two hours of pain-free sleep. Laughter gave me the escape I needed to go on with my life. My sense of humor helped reduce the amount of pain pills I needed to take. I was able to tolerate pain better because of laughter and the use of my sense of humor. Humor research has substantiated this to be true.

4 of 5 Doctors agree that 4 Out of 5 Doctors was a Washington D.C. based pop band that has nothing to do with this book, but is an interesting piece of trivia.

You do not have to roll on the floor laughing to get the benefit. I do not necessarily have to crack up heartily to tolerate some extra pain, but rather I get myself into the spirit of humor to "feel good." In my body, I feel pain daily. I also feel joy daily. Sometimes the pain is a 3 to 4 on a one to ten scale and other days it's a 7 or 8. My goal is always to increase the joy segments and decrease the pain levels. Humor does that for me.

Paul McGhee (President of The Laughter Remedy, a pioneer in humor research, AATH friend and a very humorous guy) tells a story about a minister who had been in a serious accident and had to spend several weeks in the hospital. He had a lot of pain and was given shots to reduce it. The procedure was always the same. When the pain got bad enough, the minister would ring a buzzer near his bed, and a nurse would soon come to give him the shot.

One day, he rang for the nurse and then rolled over on his side (with his back to the door), pulled his hospital gown up over his exposed backside, and waited for the nurse to come in. When he heard the door open, he pointed to his right bare buttock and said, "Why don't you give me the shot right here this time?"

After a few moments of silence, he looked up. It was a woman from his church! The minister—realizing what he had done—started laughing. He laughed so hard that tears streamed out of his eyes. As he tried to explain to the nurse what had happened, he laughed even harder. When he was finally able to tell the nurse the whole story, what do you think he noticed? His pain was gone! He didn't need the shot and didn't ask for one for another 90 minutes.

Sharing your humor makes your day and that of others better. That makes the world better.

Take time to enhance the lives of those around you. If there is a positive outcome to the interaction for someone else, then your life will be richer for it too. Humor is an equal opportunity kind of power.

One day my wife and I had argued, and when I got into bed that night, I figured she was over it. (Guys can be dumb sometimes.) As I went to cuddle with her, I heard this voice that sounded like the exorcist saying, "You're invading my legal side of the bed!"

I went back over to my designated portion of the bed and a few minutes later, she passed some gas. I said, "Your gas is invading my legal side of the bed!" With that we both laughed and cuddled to sleep. Humor can diffuse angry situations. Phyllis Diller said never go to bed angry, stay up and fight; well, I believe humor is a better alternative.

There are Personal Humor Strategies you can use to help influence yourself and others.

The strategies below are tried and true ones that I have been using most of my life to increase the humor around me.

The Silly Walk

Using yourself physically gives you a kinesthetic experience that makes the humor a physical part of you. If you have seen Monty Python's Ministry of Silly Walks, you get the idea of what I mean. Just choose some odd way of walking that amuses you. If you walk odd anyway, exaggerate it! Since my arthritis gave me a bad limp, I exaggerated it to the point of absurdity. This not only made me laugh and feel better, but also helped others get the message that I was comfortable with my illness, which eased their discomfort.

Become an Actor

Become an actor for the moment. Choose an actor or character that you find amusing and funny. I often pick Tevya from the film *Fiddler on the Roof.* This strategy is especially helpful when you find yourself becoming angry. If arguing or upset, "retake" the scene. I've done these many times, yelling, "CUT! That could have won an Academy Award! Do it again. Try repeating the same words with the same facial expression as you just did!"

The other person then becomes more conscious of their actions and behavior and can rarely repeat it as well. It becomes funny or at least less angry, bringing a new perspective on the situation. You can do it with your words and actions too. You are now an actor playing out a scene. The idea is to create a silly way to get out of the strong emotions you are feeling at that moment.

Fake Memo, Policy, etc.

This can be fun and applies to work settings and at home too. Draft a memo or policy or list of silly rules. If you watched the TV show, *The Big Bang Theory*, you know that Sheldon refers to the roommate agreement or the dating agreement often and the ludicrousness always gets a laugh. You can draft your own silly versions to take on issues or diffuse tension.

One of my favorites: *This life is a test. It is only a test. If it had been an actual life, you would have received further instructions on where to go and what to do.*

The Humor Journal

I have a humor journal that I have been keeping for many years. In it are my favorite one-liners, fake memos, stories, bumper stickers and comic scenes that I have found funny or created myself. Gather tidbits of what you find funny. You can keep them in a folder on your computer, on your phone, or in a real actual physical folder or journal.

Humor journal excerpts include:

"Why did the guy with arthritis fall down? Someone pushed him."

"Humor is in my blood. Frankly, I wish it was in this book."

"I used to be a psychiatric social worker, but I wasn't crazy about it."

During a PowerPoint presentation: This is my daughter's favorite slide:

Share Embarrassing Moments

Consider embarrassing moments. We all have them. Many are really funny. When something embarrassing happens to us, we feel mortified. If you change the way you look at these moments, you will feel much less stress when they happen and that will result in less of a negative impact on your health. This not only helps you overcome embarrassment but gives others a good laugh too.

My brother Phil shared an embarrassing situation that happened to him several years ago. He was in a store and picked up a Playboy magazine. He opened it and nudged his wife standing next him, and said, "What do you think of these?" The lady next to him wasn't his wife, but a seventy-year-old board member of the Jewish Community Center where he was the Director of Art. She looked at the picture and said, "Oh, that's nice."

When my wife and I were visiting this same brother, I had my own embarrassing moment. As you know I have psoriatic arthritis. Another chronic illness I have is … Dun dun dun… the heart break of psoriasis. Sometimes this skin affliction affects sensitive parts of the body. That night as we were going to bed, my groin started to itch. I went to the medicine cabinet and grabbed a bottle of Bactine and sprayed some on. It seemed to cool the area and I went off to bed.

Later in the night, I felt a burn in the area so I went back to the medicine cabinet for more Bactine. A few hours later, I woke up with my groin area really burning. I sprayed on more Bactine on but couldn't go back to sleep with the burn getting worse and worse. I tried to wait until morning, but finally reached the point of going crazy. Laurie awoke to my jumping up and down, holding my groin and yelling I needed to go to the hospital.

At the ER, when the clerk started asking the insurance questions, I screamed for them to kill me or knock me out. They put me in a room and a doctor finally gave me a shot. He explained that I gave myself a chemical burn with the Bactine and just kept making it worse by pouring more on. Terrible at the time, funny story now. My brother says this story always reminds him of that Jerry Lee Lewis song. *Goodness Gracious!* You know the next line.

This habit boils down to: If you can laugh at it, you can overcome it; and if you can help others to laugh at their problems, you can help them overcome them too. Humor is a positive influence on our lives. Use it daily.

Take a good look at your attitude. Do you have a positive outlook on life? Could you inspire yourself with your sense of humor? Could you inspire others? Is humor important to you? I'm hoping the answer is yes.

You may be familiar with The Good Samaritan study by Isen and Levin of the University of California at Berkeley. Subjects were people using public pay phones in malls in San Francisco and Philadelphia. (Not a recent study, obviously, but the results are always applicable.) Some subjects found a dime in the pay phone, planted there by the experimenters. Others did not.

As each subject left the phone booth, a person who was part of the experiment dropped a folder full of papers in their path. Of the eight men and eight women who had found the free dimes, six men and all eight women helped pick up the papers. Of the nine men and sixteen women who had not found a free dime, eight men and sixteen women did not stop to help pick up the papers.

Social psychologists Isen and Levin suggest that finding the dime led subjects to feel in a good mood, and feeling good leads to helping. Humor helps us feel good, maybe even more than finding a dime, and can lead to positive emotions which can lead to helping people.

Would you like to be recognized for your humorous contributions to others and yourself? It does not have to be difficult. Commit to improving your sense of humor. You are halfway through the habits already. You now see that humor is a necessity. You can easily implement some self-effacing humor and find some humor in nearly all situations. That makes you a powerful force of good in the world.

Can you commit to increasing your use of humor to increase your power of influence? You just might see miracles happen. Maybe you'll even find a dime in a pay phone.

Chapter Five:
Habit 5 -- Use humor to improve your communication

My new editing software has no thesaurus; I have no words for how upset this made me.

If necessity is the mother of invention and creativity is the father of invention, then humor must be the favorite uncle of invention.

As Oscar Wilde said, "I am so clever that sometimes I don't understand a single word of what I am saying." You don't need to be that clever, just clever enough to occasionally share humorous observations you've found by using your humorous imagination to improve your communication.

Mis-communication happens more often than Mr-Communication. The ability to clarify communication has much to do with your mental state at the time of the communication. Are you feeling happy, healthy and humorous? Are you putting into practice the tips of the previous chapters?

Improving your sense of humor truly does make you a better communicator.

We all know that we liked teachers who were funny. And bosses. And speakers. And authors. You don't have to be a slapstick or a pro jokester to insert a little humor into your interactions.

You can share a simple silly with everyone you meet. The majority of people in this country are not all that humorous. One out of every five, wouldn't you say? A survey conducted by the US census bureau has concluded that these one out of five people make up only 20% of the population.

For years at my humor seminars, I have shared funny stories that always amuse people. Some of them are Urban Legends. When people laugh with you, they listen to you. Even if your stories are golden oldies.

You may have heard of the housewife doing the laundry. She takes a basketful of dirty laundry to the basement to put in the washer and decides to strip off her own clothing to add to the load. She removes a load of clean laundry from the dryer, puts it in the basket, and starts up the basement steps when she notices her son has left his football helmet there. She picks up the helmet to take it to his room, but, having no other place to put it with both arms holding the laundry basket, she plunks it on her head.

At that moment the outside basement door opens. It is the meterman who has come to read the meters, also located in the basement. The housewife drops the basket and stands exposed in the sunlight streaming in through the open doorway. The meterman gulps, and says, "I sure hope your team wins, lady." This story dates to at least 1961, when a less scandalous version appeared in the pages of *Reader's Digest*.

Another story is about a lady who came home from the grocery store and saw her husband working under the car. All that was exposed were his legs, so in passing she reached down, unzipped his zipper, chuckled to herself, and went into the house.

Immediately she saw her husband sitting in the easy chair reading the newspaper. She cried, "Who is THAT under the car?" Her husband replied, "My mechanic." She told her husband what she'd done, and they went outside to find the mechanic lying unconscious, because when the lady unzipped his pants, he was so startled he sat up and clobbered his head under the car. Some attendees told me they recall having first heard this legendary tale as far back as the late 1950s.

Humor helps you with the hard conversations too. If you dislike or are upset with the person you're speaking to, then chances are you'll not be as interested in what he/she has to say. That makes for a less than pleasant work environment. Or household.

Here are some humor and communication tips.

Tip One: Use your humorous imagination to improve your listening skills.

Let's say that you are angry with another person you are about to speak to. This will make communication difficult. You must get out of the angry mood. Think to yourself something along the lines of. "I wonder what this person would do if cheese started pouring out of their ear?" The other person will then see you smiling and know you are open to communication. You will feel better and be more willing to listen.

Tip Two: Pretend what you are about to hear is the most important thing you will ever hear in your life. When you are that focused on someone, they will think you are the most wonderful person in the world. Try it and you may be surprised at the positive results. A psychologist conducted an experiment on a flight from NYC to LA. For the entire flight, all he did was ask questions of the passenger next to him and listened to his answers. The psychologist had a cohort waiting in LA to talk to this passenger upon arrival who was asked: "Do you know the name of the person that sat next to you?" The passenger responded, "No, but he is the most fascinating person I've ever talked to."

Tip Three: Caring is the key, and it must be genuine. Not caring enough is usually the reason for poor communication. People won't care what you have to say until they know how much you care.

The ability to communicate is one of the most important skills in life. Yet it is not always easy.

"Rock the boat, don't rock the boat baby…." This song lyric is filled with inherent contradictions. Communication can get like that.

Close your eyes. I know you can't read with your eyes closed so open them when you have to read the next instruction, but then close them again. Picture a boat in the water. Get as detailed a picture as possible in your mind. Is the boat moving? What color is it? What type of boat is it? How big is it? What is the water like?

Now here's the clincher. If someone else is thinking of a different boat, is his or her boat "wrong"? Can they both be right for each of you? Why do we get caught up with needing to have others tell us that our boat is right? This is the basis of most arguments. Instead of boats, it is our values or politics or religion. Or sports team.

We get blinders on when it comes to "our boat." Our boat consists of the baggage, judgements, projections and perceptions we give power to. These projections and perceptions hold us back from truly hearing others. Use humor to break through these barriers.

I can smile while you describe your boat. You can smile when you hear about my boat. When you reach a point when you can smile when someone else is describing their "boat," you have mastered communication. Overcoming these barriers will improve your relationships and all your interactions with others. The amount of stress in your life will decrease and the amount of health and joy will increase.

Republican, Democrat, Christian, Jew, Muslim, Buddhist, Hindu. Gay, Straight, Curvy. They're all different colored boats. One is not right, and one is not WRONG! In a salad, there are greens, reds, browns, blacks, yellows, whites. They all make the salad look and taste better. There is not a right and wrong taste. When we can embrace the differences, we can decrease the amount of judgement and prejudice in the world.

Let's respect all the boats in the world.

Take the time and do the hard work of truly listening. Listen with your mind, heart and spirit. Give the time needed to truly understand and you will save much more time than you could ever imagine. Do it with joy; you and the other party will get an added benefit.

One day while working on my master's thesis for graduate school in social work, my three-year-old daughter came into the room and asked, "Papa, can we play?"

I responded "No, honey, I'm working right now."

She wandered away disappointed. Five minutes later, she came back and asked, "Can we play now?"

Again I said no. She asked why not and I said because I have to finish this thesis so I can graduate, get a job and have money to send you to college. This seemed to satisfy her and she left again.

A few minutes later, she came back with her change purse and said, "Papa here's money for college. Can we play now?"

How do you say no to that? The answer is you can't. It's as important to take time to play as it is to take time to work on your other projects. Using a sense of humor makes everything better, including dealing with toddlers, teenagers, spouses, coworkers, everyone. Humor helps in all our communication.

Humorous listening diffuses anger. It decreases stress. It helps us become more flexible.

This will help make the world a better place for all of us. A strong humor foundation gives you the confidence to listen. We all have fears. We fear that others could influence our worldviews and we don't want them to. If you are confident and open you can go from the "Yes, but" mentality to the "Yes, and" mentality. Allow your horizons to expand, your worldview to broaden. Your life can open up. Use humor to overcome barriers to communication.

Both love and humor in communication can defuse anger and resolve conflict. Humor that comes from a place of love is humor in its highest form.

Playful humor can improve interpersonal communication. Does timing matter? Absolutely. Don't you hate it when someone answers their own questions? I do.

As stated earlier, you look for something which is humorous to you. You also need to know that your humor may not be the same as that of another. You need to take into account others' age, education level, social class, place of origin and the setting that you are in before you decide on the appropriate type of humor to use.

For example, the humor I use with my fellow PWAs (People with Arthritis) may be a little different than the type I use in other interactions.

Here are some examples from a talk I did with my fellow peeps with arthritis.

THREE LITTLE KITTENS

Three little kittens, they lost their med records, and they began to cry, "Oh, receptionist we sadly fear, our records we have lost. "

What! Lost your records, You silly kittens! Then you shall have no appointment. Mee-ow, mee-ow, mee-ow.

No, you shall have no appointment!

The three little kittens, they found their records, and they began to cry, "Oh, receptionist, see here, see here. Our records we have found."

Hand me your records, you happy kittens, and you shall have an appointment, Purr-r, purr-r, purr-r, and you shall have an appointment,

The three little kittens gave over their records

And got an appointment

...four months later

Rub a dub dub

Rub a dub dub

Three men soaking in a tub

And who has arthritis here?

The butcher, the baker, the candlestick maker

Because arthritis does not discriminate when it comes to occupations

SIMPLE SIMON

Simple Simon met a pieman,

while he had a flare

Says Simple Simon to the pieman,

"I really need a chair."

Says the pieman to Simple Simon,

"You're too young to have arthritis"

You can do the same with common examples in your life. When I did a talk for the American Case Management Asssociation, I used the same concept, but tweaked my wording for this different group of people who work in hospital settings.

Old King Cole

Old King Cole

walked with his IV Pole

waiting for discharge was he;

He called for his case manager

And he called for his ride

but his ride had to wait til he'd pee.

Humor breaks the ice, bonds us, and can also enhance your powers of persuasion. In *The Adventures of Tom Sawyer*, you probably recall the fence painting scene. Tom tricks another boy into thinking that white washing his fence – the thing that he doesn't want to do – is fun. Tom is then able to spend the afternoon goofing off. Tom even gets the boy to pay him for the "privilege" of painting.

Using humor may not get anyone to do your chores, but it can make colleagues and coworkers do their tasks with more enjoyment, and certainly can help you get through your day. Start paying attention (and implementing the other humor habits) and you will see many instances where humor has helped a situation.

Communication is critical in any relationship, be it at work or at home, so be sure to infuse humor in your conversations. Who knows, you might just discover that your spouse and your kids actually listen to you at dinner time.

Chapter Six

Habit Six – Humorize with your humor spirit

To humorize is to make something humorous. You have the ability, when you are in a poor mood (or any mood), to merely think about something funny and begin to feel better. To humorize is making something humorous by seeing it through the eyes of your humor spirit.

Of course, your humor spirit doesn't have eyes, but it is a part of your soul. Laughter normally occurs unconsciously. We can, however, purposely inhibit it.

To use your humor spirit is to use your ability to consciously produce laughter. Laughter is largely still a mystery. We have only just begun to explore this uncharted realm of the mind.

I came up with a term I call "humorgy," but explaining it is not easy. It is taking a universal, but very personal experience and trying to put into words something felt on a spiritual level in addition to its physiological, psychological, social and emotional levels.

You no longer distinguish your humor self from your spiritual self. They are one in the same. Like mixing flavored food coloring with water, once done the particles cannot be separated out.

You've colored and flavored your spirit with your humor, enhancing it, giving you a better ability to infuse humor into the world, to appreciate love, hope, joy and all the positive emotions. You see that judging is useless, revenge is futile, resistance to the spirit of humor is futile, and arguing with a two-year-old is futile. Life, yours and everyone you come in contact with, is a gift. With your humorgy, you can appreciate everyone's boat.

Imagine being able to see something from your perspective and from an opposing perspective at the same time. With humorgy you can do that. It's like Tevya in *Fiddler on the Roof*, when he sees one perspective and another and agrees they are both right and then hears a third opinion. For example:

Person One: "Why should I break my head about the outside world? Let the outside world break its own head.

Tevya: "Well put! He is right. As the Good Book says, "If you spit in the air, it lands in your face."

Person Two: "Nonsense. You can't close your eyes to what's happening in the world.

Tevya: "He is right."

Person Three: "He's right and he's right? They can't both be right."

Tevya: "You know, you are also right!"

If you know Star Wars, you know about The Force. Humorgy is the source of the Humor Force. In Star Wars, they measured young Anakin's midi-chlorians and they were "off the scales." Though there is some research that points to a possible "humor" gene, for now we will be satisfied with implementing our humor habits to increase our health and happiness.

When you increase your humor, you help yourself and you help others. Liken it to putting humor in the air and we all breathe the same air. Also know that there is a Humor Force, but we don't force it on anyone.

If you have two cups and one has a hole in it, which would you put water in? Putting water in the cup with the hole is like trying to pour your opinions into another person. What you say will just flow right on out.

We all do this every day. I am not talking about sharing your opinions, I'm talking about trying to force your opinions (your colored flavored water) into another person's cup (spirit). "My faith is better than your faith." "My values are superior to yours." "My political party is better than yours." "My opinions are more valid yours." "My cup is more cuppier than yours."

It's all nonsense. Rather than try to change the other person, share your cup of colored water with them. Let them taste your flavor. Don't pour your flavor in their cup!

Humorgy allows one to appreciate their own flavor AND taste favorite flavors of others.

You also allow in new flavor combinations. We are all constantly learning. Humor helps us to do so.

By combining humor with all other aspects of life, your entire lifestyle can change. Maybe you have physical pain, maybe you have emotional pain. To utilize your humorgy is to have the ability to look at yourself and pull your pain out of the driver's seat and place it in the back seat. The greater your pain, the greater your ability to use humorgy. This is why some people who are extremely funny have overcome extreme tragedies in their life.

Take your spiritual self, your physical self, your mental self, your social self, your economic self, and political self. And your fish self or your self-fishes. When you can take all parts of yourself and add the spirit of humor, you experience wholeness in a way that can't be described, only felt. Be open to that and you'll have humorgy, the Humor Spirit.

With humorgy you see the whole, which diminishes prejudice, judgement, and all negative aspects of life. Humor reveals the interconnection between all of us. It is an ideal that we can all strive to reach.

Humorgy can be used for self-control. Humorous thoughts protect you from getting sucked into the vacuum cleaner of dirt-filled negative thoughts including thoughts of hate, depression, envy, greed, and jealousy.

My wife looked at the word "humorgy" and said "Gee, that looks like a combination of humor and orgy." She may be right. A humor-orgy. When you define the term orgy by its meaning of excess in something to satisfy an inordinate appetite or craving, it fits. A humor orgy or humorgy is an unending craving for humor. If you must be addicted to something, I recommend an addiction to humor. It is one of the only addictions that can alter your consciousness, without damaging your health. In fact, it can improve your health.

A concept close to humorgy is "Psychoneurospirituimmunology." This made-up word is based on the actual word psychoneuroimmunology (PNI). I added spirit to this word according to Daniel Webster's Guide on how to make up words. (The guide doesn't exist, I made that up too.).

The spiritual component is not taken into consideration in psychoneuroimmunology (PNI), but spirit is an important component, and deserves a part in defining any holistic approach to healing.

PNI defines the communication links and relationships between our emotional experience and our immune response as mediated by the neurological system. Robert Ader in 1980, a psychiatrist on the faculty at the University of Rochester, first used the term in the study of the interactions among the behavioral, neural and endocrine (or neuroendocrine), and immunological processes of adaptation.

The central premise is that homeostasis is an integrated process involving interactions among the nervous, endocrine and immune systems as well as the thermostat in your "home" body. In plain English: it's the mind, body, spirit connections, but researchers haven't found a way to put the spirit under a microscope yet, so they leave that part out.

Our behaviors and thoughts can affect and modify immune functions. Scientists are discovering what yogis have known for centuries. We can control our heart rate, our blood pressure, our body heat, our digestion and a whole bunch of other previously thought involuntary body functions of our autonomic system. In addition, Yogi has also known that picnic baskets in National Parks are one of the most wonderful things in life. Boos Boos would also agree with this.

Where does the spiritual aspect fit in? There is not much literature on this topic. There is no definitive definition of spiritual humor. It is as diverse as the number of religious and spiritual orders in the universe. This makes it difficult to measure. It's not like economics where you can say 84% of struggling or lost souls are due to lack of humor, etc.

I have a humorous relationship with what I call "the master of the universe." It is not sacrilegious but highly religious to me to jest with "the master of the universe." It's obvious he/she has a sense of humor or I would never have been created. My life is a joke and I mean that in the most sacred way.

There are so many times in life that we run across examples of the cosmic joke. One example is the teeth on the steering wheel story. When I got to the church that morning to give the humor and spirituality talk, I told the story of what happened on the way. At the end of my talk on that rainy cloudy day, I said to the congregation, "You know, every once in a while, we get confirmation from above that we are doing what we should be doing." Just then BAM! A huge thunder crack sounded. I looked up and said, "THANK YOU!"

There are cues from the humor spirit all the time. We just have to notice them. There have been a few different times I have returned from overseas travel and my best friend, David, picked me up at the airport. Each time we got in the car David put the radio on and the song "The Boys Are Back in Town" by Thin Lizzy would be playing on the radio. I see that as a nod from the humor spirit.

Whether you believe in a higher power or not, it's hard to deny that there is something going on and it's funny too. Funny and strange are often used interchangeably. I'm a funny guy. I'm also a strange guy. People that think I'm strange don't realize I'm just being funny and people that think I'm being funny don't realize I'm strange.

As a spiritual being, I am having fun trying to figure out the unfathomable while in this body. How can you live life as a drudge when there is such a limited time on this planet? If I had a thousand years, I'd be serious for maybe a hundred years, but that's not the case.

The greatest definition I have found for spiritual humor is in the movie "The Meaning of Life" by Monty Python. Eric Idle sings "The Galaxy Song" that is the best "revelation" of the spiritual explanation to the phrase "the cosmic joke of the universe." The laugh comes at the end when we are all caught with the same thought that John Cleese says out loud: "Kind of makes you feel small, doesn't it."

We laugh because we are busted. He's read our mind and stripped away a universal secret that human beings have. We feel insignificant compared to the universe. The contradiction is that as small as we feel, we also feel that we have universal potential at the same time to create great outcomes that can affect our universe as well.

We are the heroes of our own lives. We all also have heroes that reflect and "prove" to us that this is true. I'm sure you have examples in your own life.

Let me don my teacher hat and share the integral parts of "Psychoneurospirituimmunology:"

1. Our thought process: "I am great and can overcome obstacles."

2. Our physical body: "I feel healing energy in my body."

3. Our nervous system: "I feel warm and comfortable."

4. Our spiritual self: "I have a reason for being here."

We are human beings. We have a potential for a high level of humorgy, that is greater than the sum of each of these separate individual parts. We don't have to fully understand it, just accept it and be grateful.

There is a story about a Texas billionaire who held a big bash every year. He would always have some outrageous event to highlight the evening. One year he filled his Olympic-sized swimming pool full of man-eating (and women-eating) alligators and announced, "Anyone who dares to swim the length of this pool and survives to make it out the other side can have either a million dollars, half my estate, or the hand of my daughter in marriage."

With that everyone heard a splash at the end of the pool. A man was swimming, kicking and punching alligators. Amazingly, he made it out alive on the other side.

"Do you want a million dollars?" asked the billionaire.

"No!" the man replied.

"Do you want half my estate?"

The man responded, "Of course not."

The billionaire said, "I suppose you want my daughter's hand?"

"NO! What would I do with your daughter's hand?"

The billionaire, frustrated at this point said, "Well, what do you want?"

The man replied: "I want to find the SOB who pushed me in the pool!"

In everyone's life there comes a time when we find ourselves in that pool. Whether we're pushed in, fall in, or choose to jump in doesn't matter much. The important thing is to find a way out before drowning or being eaten alive. Humorgy is your life jacket to help you survive while in the pool and the ladder to pull you out.

Additional parts of the humorgy whole are inherited traits, personal experiences and the influence of your environment. Also, chicken wings, but they don't play a very big part. As mentioned earlier in this chapter, there is research that points to something in our DNA that helps to shape our sense of humor and our ability to tap into our positive emotions. Those with a genetic variant of the gene 5-HTTLPR (serotonin-transporter-linked polymorphic region) are more likely to show positive expressions, including laughing and smiling. See Appendix B for a link with more information.

Our experiences also have an influence. My parents had a great sense of humor, although my mother had tendencies towards sarcasm, which can be positive or negative, depending on the context. Where you grow up and live also has an impact. If you were raised in a home where at dinner you could joke and laugh and make balls out of the mashed potatoes, like at my house, you are more likely to be more comfortable with using humor at the dinner table. If you were raised in a home where dinner was a sacred time of grace and gratitude, then you may have a little more difficulty being comfortable sharing humor over dinner. One isn't right, and one isn't wrong; this simply represents different life experiences, different boats.

Humorgy helps fuel our imagination and flights of fantasy - the ability to create in our mind actions, scenes and stories that don't exist in what we call reality.

In the moment that the Humor Force takes over, you go into the witness state of humorgy. This means getting out of yourself to see the situation from a different perspective. Humor can give you this amazing power to do just that, to see through humorgy filtered eyes with a new, fresh, better, more positive perspective.

When you're able to do that, life gets a whole lot better.

Chapter Seven
Habit Seven – Act like a humorous, happy, healthy person.

Mark Twain said, "Humor is the great thing, the saving thing after all. The minute it crops up, all our hardnesses yield, all our irritations, and resentments flit away, and a sunny spirit takes their place."

You are on your journey to becoming a more humorous, happy and healthy person. Use your advanced humor powers to help yourself and others further improve both yours and others' sense of humor. Take more time to laugh, watch a comedy, see some stand up, act silly, etc. Implement all of these habits you just read about.

This last habit is not exactly "fake it until you make it." When I say, "act like a humorous person," I mean embrace the idea that you are becoming more humorous. There is a huge difference between pretending and acting as if.

Many years ago, when I was an Executive National Sales Director for Flashnet Marketing, I met John Milton Fogg (author and networking expert) at a training he did for the executives of our company. He provided me with an a-ha moment because of his explanation of the word belief.

When you study the root of the word belief, you gain greater understanding of its depth and meaning. The true definition of belief will give you a glimpse into why our attitudes and beliefs are so powerful. The word belief comes from two words: Be and lief.

Be comes from being, a state of existence. "To Be or Not to Be." In other words, being alive. The second word lief comes from the Indo-European word leubh which means – love. So, when you put that together it changes the entire idea of the word belief.

Belief means to be in love with. My belief or what I am in love with is the idea that humor has the power to transform the world.

Belief doesn't mean you have to know that is true for a fact, all you must do is be in love with the idea that it can be true. A true belief is something that resonates in your heart, mind and soul.

Be in love with the idea that the creator of the world exists in whatever form you choose to believe in. Be in love with the idea that you have a co-operative part and influence in that master plan created by the creator of the universe.

Have the belief that humor matters deeply and can change your health and happiness. Be in love with the idea!

Think about this in relation to the role humor plays in your life. Instead of waiting for the proof that humor will enhance your health, happiness and humor abilities, you just need to start using it more and look through your humor-filtered glasses because you love the notion that humor can have these positive effects.

When you believe in your spouse, your children, your friends, humanity in general, what you are really saying is you love them or are in love with the idea that you love them.

If you love this idea, you will act as if. Not only will you act as if, you will also attract others with the same belief.

This is one of the reasons I joined AATH - the Association for Applied and Therapeutic Humor. I wanted to be around like-minded people. The result is I now have connections with the greatest therapeutic humor practitioners in the world with the same passion for humor.

Be in love with the idea that you are becoming more humorous, that your sense of humor is strengthening every day. Think of your favorite sauce. My favorites are honey barbecue sauce and teriyaki sauce. When I make a mix and spread it on chicken, and cook it well, there is no better taste in the world.

How do you think you taste to others? Are you bitter, sweet, strong, mild, hot, salty? What is your "sauce"?

Our sauce is never done. We keep changing and tweaking and improving our whole lives. Adding ingredients, leaving behind others. Sometimes we add too much of one and are sorry. Sometimes we are out of the one ingredient we want the most. By constantly tasting and testing, we perfect ourselves.

Your "sauce" is how you taste to yourself and others. There is not just one sauce. We have:

Physical Sauce

Spiritual Sauce

Mental sauce

Social Sauce

Mix all these together and you'll have your sense of humor or "sauce" of humor.

Your taste in humor is an outward expression of your inner being. A person with a low sense of humor does not command much of a presence to others, whereas someone who values their sense of humor and the humor of others is like an old soul whose presence is noticed by all they encounter.

The Physical Sauce is flavored by your daily physical activities, your hygiene, driving time in the car, the way you move and the amount of physical activity you do on a regular basis. Overstressing your body (too much exercising), under-stressing your body (not enough exercise) or overindulging your body (too much eating or too much other physical pleasures) are detrimental to this sauce. A happy medium in between is recommended, with some exercise and some pleasures too.

As Buddha said, always take the Middle Road. When he was on the Middle Road, he stopped at a hot dog stand and said, "Make me one with everything." The vendor made him one with everything and said, "That'll be $2.00. Buddha gave him a $5.00 bill. The vendor smiled and sat back down. Buddha asked, "Where's my change?" The hot dog vendor replied, "Change must come from within."

We now know that humor and avoiding rabid dogs are both good preventative health measures. We're also aware of the stress response or the "fight or flight syndrome" and how detrimental it can be to our physical health.

You've felt the fight or flight stress response. Your heart starts to race. Your blood pressure goes up. Stomach acids increase. The mouth goes dry. Adrenaline amounts rise to give the body more fuel and energy. Your ability to digest food stops so that more blood can flow to muscles. Muscle tension increases. Perspiration increases to cool the body and help companies sell more anti-perspirants. The spleen releases stored blood cells and cortisol, a blood-clotting agent; and lactic acid rushes to the muscles for added strength. The liver releases glucose for energy. Your breathing becomes shallower, your personality becomes shallower, and your chances of winning the lottery decreases... it's just a terrible mess all around!

If stress continues to go unchecked for any period, eventually your resistance to disease and infections will be lowered, your health will be in jeopardy and I'm not talking Alex Trebek. There are a lot of negative effects to that stress. When that high level of stress occurs and heart rate's increased and muscles become tense, adrenalin flows through the blood, there's something we need to do to counteract that, so we don't have a heart attack or some other negative health event. There's many ways to do that.

Meditation can induce a relaxation response, as can spending time in nature. The humorous person uses their humorgy (humor spirit) and laughter as the greatest antidote. There are no bad side effects and it's very good for you. Well, there might be one side effect if you laugh too hard, but rubber panties will solve that one.

Think about when you have a hearty laugh. You're just cracking up and taking deep breaths. When you're laughing like that, you are oxygenating your blood. You're breathing much deeper than normal, removing residual air that may have been stuck in your lungs since Miley Cyrus played Miley Stewart on Hannah Montana.

Let's get gross for a second. People who are bed bound and can't exercise can use hearty laughter to remove mucous plugs that would otherwise only be removed with the help of a respiratory treatment. If you had a choice between someone pounding hard on you like a drum or laughing hard, which would you choose?

Coughing up phlegm is very good for you, but very bad to talk about. I am repulsed by phlegm. It makes me sick to even write this. I'd rather see a bucket of blood than a teaspoon of phlegm. I'm getting dry heaves, so let's quickly change the subject.

Your blood pressure initially shoots up during your laughter, but afterwards decreases below normal for a while. Research shows that people who laugh hearty on a regular basis have lower standing blood pressures than the average population.

My blood pressure is extremely low. It is due to taking too much blood pressure medication, (kidding), but laughter works better. Laughter also decreases your muscle tension. There's evidence that laughter stimulates the production of catecholamines, the alertness hormones, and laughter may even cause the release of endorphins into the brain, which are natural pain killers (that look like dolphins under the microscope thus the name endorphins).

Endorphins are a type of neuropeptide, which means they may be affected by the phases of the moon, because the moon commonly affects "tides." These endorphins work "porpoisely" to improve your ability to tolerate pain. You've heard of the runner's high. There are certain things that induce this altered state and laughter is one of them and much less strenuous than running a marathon.

There is no doubt that being a humorous person improves your health by having positive thoughts daily. How do you define physical health? Endurance, flexibility and strength?

I have severe arthritis. Am I healthy? You bet your sweet hollandaise sauce I am. My physical health is defined by what I can do within the limitations of my physical body. I can exercise, eat right. I said I can, not that I always do.

I can transcend this body in other ways, but physically I must abide by the laws of nature and live within the shell I have. Still this shell took me on a 115-mile bike ride, a 50-mile unicycle ride, and a 20-mile swim. Well, the twenty-mile swim was a year of swimming laps, but still with the miracle of "reframing," I can say I swam twenty miles. And you can too! If you walk around your block once every day, you can say that you have done a marathon. It may take you a year, but hey "who cares?" (as my mother-in-law was fond of saying.)

The Spiritual Sauce is your spirit, your true essence. Whether born with a humorous spirit or that of Ebenezer Scrooge, your humorous nature can always be developed or changed, just like Ebenezer. Indecently, for you trivia buffs Ebenezer derives from the Hebrew: stone of help. (Who would name their kid Ebenezer anyway?) (If your name is Ebenezer, please contact me and I promise I will do something special for you if you feel insulted.)

Meditation and prayer and quiet time to calm the spirit can be helpful. The type of meditation or prayer doesn't matter. If you feel more comfortable with a mantra to chant, I recommend, "Hey Moe" or "WOOP WOOP WOOP." This will really help your spiritual humor emerge.

I have a hard time separating my humor from my spirituality. They are two sides of the same coin. It is a gold coin from the Roman era with a picture of Nixon on one side and Moses on the other. My purpose is to use my humorous side to inspire others. That in turn fuels my passion to continue spreading the message about humor's positive qualities.

Through the spirit of laughter, we feel and know that we are connected to each other. Our sense of humor helps to reveal that inner connection we have with each other.

The Mental Sauce is important too. My humor journal is one source that helps me enhance the taste of this sauce. It's important to have private humor time. Humor is not only meant to be shared with others, it's meant to be shared with yourself. Humor fantasies, looking in the mirror and making funny faces, dancing in the elevator, biting the steering wheel in the car are all flavors of the mental sauce.

My sense of humor improved after my arthritis diagnosis. My ability to use humor to cope improved. With every event or situation, psychologically, we know it's not the event that causes the stress, it's how we perceive it. If you can use humor to change the way you perceive a situation, you're going to have a psychological benefit from doing that.

By sustaining a more positive mood and reducing the amount of time spent in a state of anger, anxiety or depression, you can play an active role in mobilizing your body's own health and healing forces. Your emotional state begins working for you, rather than against.

The Social Sauce is a key ingredient. Think about your relationships with others. Who are your friends? One thing we all notice is that we usually spend time with people who we can laugh with and have a joyful time with. If you're not having joy with the people you interact with a daily basis, this sauce will get bitter. Every laugh and smile add sweetness to this sauce. A well-timed humorous observation will release tension and enhance the interactions of any group.

My first week of work at University Medical Center was as a trauma social worker was during a holiday week in December. I had dealt with child deaths, gunshot wounds, motor vehicle accidents. It was a bad week. At the first social work meaning I attended, my manager asked, "So, David, how was your first week of work?"

Words couldn't describe the hell of that week, so I didn't bother to respond by speaking. Instead I just looked at him and fell off my chair and collapsed on the floor. Most people chuckled and after the meeting, many came up to me and said, "Hey David, thanks for making our usually boring meeting a little lighter."

I felt good about that. My humor helped me feel better about myself. My self-confidence improved. And humor helped my co-workers too.

Please take the time to let humor help you feel better too. Humor has a tremendous ripple effect. Act like a humorous, happy, healthy person. You are.

Chapter Seven Point Five
The ½ Habit

Mastering your thoughts

This half habit "enhances the flavor" of the humor sauce. This half habit refers to inner thought.

Since you started reading this book, you've been talking to yourself. Hey, it's okay. Everyone does it. You may even be thinking to yourself right now, "Gee, I'm talking to myself."

Notice your thoughts. Don't let a common negative thought rule your life, as in, "My life sucks." Rather let this thought be replaced and be a steady guide: "My life not only doesn't suck, but I enjoy chocolate as well."

Think of the future you, one year from now. Looking back, would you rather have ruminated on 21,900,000 negative thoughts that stressed you out and affected your health, well-being, attitude, feelings and behaviors? OR would you rather have cut your negative thoughts in half and ruminated on only 10,950,000 negative thoughts?

You may be thinking, "Hey David, where'd you come up with those numbers?" Consider that on average, we have about 60,000 thoughts per day. Multiply that by 365 days (if you live on Earth, of course; if you live on Mercury it's only 88 days, so you may wish to consider moving there). So do the math. You can borrow my calculator.

I downgraded this habit to one half its strength because you don't need to do this one hundred percent of the time for it to be effective. Also the title of "8 Habits" just doesn't sound as fun.

This half habit can be quite a challenge. Our mind is very busy all the time. Even if we're physically lazy, our mind is busy churning negative thoughts out about how lazy we are. It's human nature to have negative thoughts and times when we feel down. It is impossible to have only positive thoughts all the time. Therefore, if you master it half the time, you'll feel twice as good and likely feel twice as healthy! If you can change just half of your negative thoughts, you'll be happier, healthier and sexier.

Start right now playing with examples of how you can change a negative thought to one that feels better.

"Nobody likes me" can change to

"There are still 7.6 billion people I haven't met yet, so there's still hope."

"My body looks gross" can change to

"Compared to what I'll look like in 40 years, I don't look too bad."

"People think I'm boring" can change to

"People who think I'm boring don't really know me. Or are they my kids?"

It might not be easy to abruptly just stop a negative habit or negative thoughts. They must be replaced. We must consciously think about it at first. Negative self-talk statements make us feel sad or angry and the result is increased stress and tension. When we notice our thoughts we can switch them to something that feels better, in every way.

When you awake tomorrow, what kind of day will it be? It's your choice. Just as we clothe ourselves based on the weather, we clothe our thoughts based on how we're feeling. If I'm feeling negative, I can catch myself if I try.

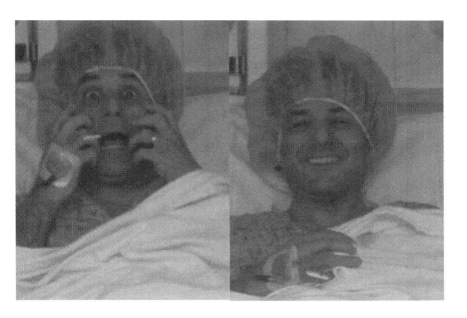

Two choices on how to face surgery, which to choose?

Just like with clothing, I can replace my negative bra with a joyful one. Okay, I don't wear a bra, but if I keep eating like I have the past month, I might have to soon. Changing thoughts from negative to positive takes a conscious effort to become more aware of our internal conversations. Like right now I'm writing and while I'm writing I'm thinking I want people to get more out of this book. I want it to be valuable.

I can go down the route of "I don't know what I'm doing and I am not a good writer" OR I can replace that negative thought with "I am simply trying to convey some good information and I trust the end result will help some people."

Have you found yourself facing one challenging situation after another, posing a threat to your happiness, hopefulness, and peace of mind? Would you like to find another way to deal with those challenging situations? All of us at one time or another thought that a situation we were in was bad, but then it turned out to be much better than we expected.

Humor is the pearl in the oyster of life, we all need a little sand in contrast to appreciate that pearl that much more.

I have a shoe box I keep at home. It's over 30 years old and filled with over 40 letters of rejection from social services jobs I applied for, but was rejected from, perhaps due to my arthritis? Bad luck? Negative thoughts? I didn't know, but what I did know was that someday I would get a job in the social service field that I loved and would be able to show others those rejection letters and say "See, if you're determined and don't give up, things will be just great!"

Had I not been rejected from all those social service jobs I applied for, I would not have thought of applying for Vocational Rehabilitation. The result was being told that due to my severe arthritis I qualified for full vocational rehabilitation benefits. I was asked if I could be anything what would I want to be? I answered a social worker and Voc Rehab paid for me to go to Graduate School for my master's in social work.

Had I not gotten arthritis, I would not have done my 50-mile unicycle ride fundraiser for the Arthritis Foundation raising tons of money for them and becoming an inspiration to children and young adults with the disease. My first standing ovation was when I spoke at an Arthritis Foundation National Hero Overcoming Arthritis event in Atlanta. My inspirational speech launched my professional speaking career, and later inspired me to write my first book.

Had I not been involved in the horrible Tucson Shooting Tragedy, I would not have been able to work with the victims and families, improve my therapeutic skills in crisis intervention and meet President Obama and First Lady Michelle Obama.

Working with the victims, we focused on anything positive that could possibly come out of such a horrible situation. Many were able to find some positives and develop stronger coping skills for their own personal development. One newspaper quoted me as saying, "People are like sponges, they can only absorb so much before they are saturated and can't take any more." Unfortunately, they never finished the quote. My next sentence was "Humor can be used as a tool to squeeze that sponge and allow some of the stress to pour out."

Had I not worked at the Phoenix VA as Chief of Social Work, I would not have enhanced my therapeutic humor skills in trauma informed care, which gave me the ability to enhance my cognitive processing therapy with therapeutic humor which benefits Veterans with PTSD. I even had the opportunity to do Humor Consults for Veterans interested in improving their sense of humor as a coping skill.

While working there, I recall one therapy group for combat veterans with PTSD. The goal of the group was to learn to better cope with the PTSD. It was the first session and I asked them all to introduce themselves and share something, like a favorite pet, how many children or grandchildren, a favorite food or hobby, etc. As we went around the room, the veterans became more relaxed and seemed to like getting to know each other until one guy caused an awkward moment.

He said, "Hi, my name is John and I saw my best buddy have his legs blown off right in front of me." The group became silent. After a few distressing moments, I said "Well, I was hoping you'd share something a little more traumatic and personal about yourself."

The group, including John, began to laugh and the uncomfortable moment dissipated. I followed with "John, I appreciate that you shared this life experience with us and over the next 12 weeks, we'll be delving deeper into how all of us can better cope with our traumatic experiences."

You may know the story I liked telling my children about an old farmer. One day his horse ran away. His neighbor said, "Such bad luck." The farmer replied, "We don't know, we'll see." The next morning the horse returned, bringing with it three other wild horses. "How wonderful," the neighbor said. "We don't know, we'll see," the old man replied. The following day, his son tried to ride one of the untamed horses, was thrown, and broke his leg. The neighbor again said, "Such bad luck." "We don't know, we'll see," answered the farmer. The day after, military officials came to the village to draft young men into the army. Seeing that the son's leg was broken, they passed him by. The neighbor congratulated the farmer on how well things had turned out. "We don't know, we'll see" said the farmer. And so it goes.

What do you see? Will you look for the good in every challenging situation that occurs to you? Will you change your life by changing your thinking?

My arthritis pain is physical, but psychological issues such as depression, anxiety, anger, substance abuse and poor coping skills influence our experiences of pain. Your attitude about pain and its treatment can influence your attitude about humor and your attitude about humor can influence your attitude about pain.

I can't promise a cure for pain or fear, but I support your hopes for a better quality of life. Any long-lasting improvements you can make depend more upon what you can do for yourself than on what others can do for you. I used humor to test my own limits. Humor helped me move away from being a passive victim of pain to an active participant in recovery.

When overwhelmed by negative thoughts. the first task is to decide if and when to do something about it. Once you decide that you MUST do something different, it's time to take your first steps. Humor is a tool and for some it can be used to take those first steps in recovery.

Much of our struggle relates to our self-doubts. Negative thinkers are stuck in an unhealthy balance of thoughts that are self-restrictive. Hesitation is unavoidable. Generating positive humorous thoughts is a continuous and ongoing process.

How willing are you to engage in self-management of your thoughts? Are you ready to change? Do you see the need to change? Have you weighed the pros and cons? Do you know how much they weigh? Do you have a scale and is it digital or the old needle one that you never really know if it's accurate or not? You can use your humor scale to weigh your thoughts and ensure more positive ones come out than negative ones.

I am optimistic that you can do so, because you are still here reading.

Now it's time for actions. These actions can become habits if repeated enough and then maintained. Even if you relapse into negative thinking, you've already overcome your first hurdle if you've taken positive steps. Reward yourself for positive actions and when your negative thoughts surface, think to yourself "We don't know, we'll see." Then try to switch on the positive again. If relapsing, ask yourself: What do you think the problem is and why? What are you willing to try at this point?

If I had a poor sense of humor, I would have died a long time ago, either intentionally or by destructive behaviors. I can't speak for you, but I know humor pulled me out of a pit of darkness and rose me up to the brightest of lights.

That is the power of humor. The beauty of it is that it is free and available to all. No waiting in line, no forms to fill out. It's yours. Will you take it and use it?

Chapter Eight
Putting Habits Into Practice

Ten years after psoriatic arthritis seized many of my joints and changed my self-image from "Wonderman" to "Whimperman," I entered the El Tour de Tucson, a 115-mile bicycle race around the perimeter of Tucson, Arizona and an Arthritis Foundation fund-raising event.

I had no idea how far I could really go and if I could make it to the finish line but I did. In a ceremony that evening, I received the "Jim Elliott Inspirational Award," named for a man with epilepsy who holds the record for bicycling the longest distance in twenty-four hours.

This award is presented to an individual whom society often considers to be unable to participate in an event such as El Tour. This award acknowledges the courage, discipline and determination of the recipient. In other words, this award goes to someone with a chronic illness, labeled as "disabled," and not considered the type of person able to compete against "normal, healthy" individuals.

I won the Award and Jim Elliot himself presented it to me. I told him I don't deserve this award, but I have arthritis and I don't deserve that either. He laughed.

I also received a silver medal. (It wasn't really made of silver). The children, teens and young adults with arthritis saw that this could be them standing there receiving this. I was a living example that they had a future; arthritis was not their only defining feature. They could accomplish great goals despite having arthritis. Hope, faith, love and joy were with me that day, but more than all that, my humor spirit was with me and helped keep me going as it still does to this day.

After the event, I received media attention due to my accomplishment. TV, radio and newspapers all said how the following year I would be going for the gold. The next year on my first training ride, I had to call Laurie to pick me up after going just a couple miles. My knee was filling with fluid and my back was in excruciating pain, preventing me from even going a couple miles on the bike.

This is when the ego typically gets involved. Here I was supposedly the inspirational example, the "Jim Elliot Inspirational Award winner," the one who overcomes all obstacles. I was touted as the one who would cross the finish line with a gold medal and I couldn't even ride a couple miles.

The optimistic, humor-powered David was listening to the negative thoughts in his head and was feeling depressed. At this point, when our thoughts stress us out, we usually get very concrete. Either I go for the gold or don't. I felt my only choice was to give up. This type of thinking is self-defeating.

I needed to use my humor spirit to come up with an alternative. Maybe I could secretly hide a motor under a blanket on the bike, or maybe I could use a fishing pole and hook another bike-rider and catch a free ride. Maybe I could buy a giant magnet and get pulled by another rider. As soon as the humor spirit takes over, you go into the creative mode. I entered the realm of humorgy.

It was in this realm that I came up with a solution that allowed me to feel good about not riding the bike in the next El Tour and remaining physically active. As I was brainstorming silly ideas, this thought-process led my humor spirit to suggest I ride my unicycle instead. In grad school I used my unicycle to get around the huge ASU campus. I could barely walk 100 feet at the time, but I could unicycle long distances, keeping the weight off my partially fused and painful ankles.

Now ten years after graduation, I got back on the unicycle, kind of as a joke, but found a mile later, I didn't have the pain in my back and knees that I had experienced on my bike. My back was straight, and the range of motion required for riding a unicycle is much less, so my knees were less stressed. With humorgy and the humor spirit, you can trick yourself.

My goal was to ride 25 miles on a unicycle in the El Tour de Tucson. The miles went by slowly and painfully. Fighting the cold, harsh wind in my face, almost blowing me off the unicycle, and barely having enough strength to stay on the unicycle, I continued.

At Mile 7, the pain in my back got worse. I ignored it. At Mile 12, my right knee and left ankle joined the pain brigade and I could no longer ignore my sore back. I told myself "Okay self. I'll just do 15 miles today. It is a modest and obtainable goal. At 15 miles, I decided to continue for "just a few more miles." This tricking myself went on for hours, thinking "Okay, I'll do one more mile and quit."

At forty-eight miles, my body told me I was done. My humor spirit told me I wasn't. It said, "Go a couple more miles and you can laugh about this and tell stories to your grandchildren for the rest of your life."

I imagined myself with my future grandson saying, "Did I ever tell you the story of how I rode 50 miles on a unicycle against a cold brisk wind?" "Yeah, Grandpa, only a hundred times!"

Thoughts of the future old me bragging about this ride gave me a smile and gave me the strength to continue a little further. These positive thoughts bolstered my will. Knowing that the fundraiser was for the Arthritis Foundation and would benefit children with arthritis was another incentive. I also liked the idea of being an inspiration to these kids. The other "trick" was to call upon the spiritual strength of my own father.

Upon reaching the point of finally quitting, I looked up to the sky and thought of my father and his iron will and prayed for some of that will and the strength to continue this journey. Suddenly the wind, which was almost blowing me over, stopped. It was just the reprieve I needed to continue.

I tricked myself into riding my unicycle 50 miles in 6 hours and 59 minutes. Yes, you can trick yourself into accomplishing more than you could ever dream possible. To do this you must use the compelling combination of humor, positive thinking, tricking the mind, connecting to your will, connecting with your purpose in life and melding that with your personal belief system whether it be a connection with the spirit of the creator or faith in the love of our human race.

Your will is another part of humorgy / humor spirit. Your will gives you the ability to stretch yourself just a little beyond what you believe to be your limits. Humor can help strengthen your will through the half habit of positive self-talk.

One of the reasons I was able to complete my fifty-mile unicycle ride was due to spiritual strength. Humor plays a part in spiritual strength and so do my parents Israel and Rose Jacobson and the religion of my parents, which has given me the feeling of standing on the heads of giants. These giants don't particularly like having their heads stood on but understand why their heads are being stood on.

We all have countless generations of spiritual tradition that come before us and support us in times of adversity. This is the kind of help that can't be measured scientifically but still plays a part in completing any task that may seem insurmountable or unobtainable.

Even though I was young when my father died, he has continued to be an influence in my life. Israel Jacobson was one of the most decorated war veterans of World War II, a fearless, tough little guy with Herculean strength and will, who stood 5' 2 ½.

My father was a master of humorgy. When he entered a room it never went unnoticed. Humorgy is related to charisma, another word hard to define, but understood. We know what we mean when we say, "That guy has got charisma!" The common element between charisma and humor is magnetism. People are attracted to the humorous/charismatic personality. That kind of humor and spirit lives on, and continues to be an inspirational force. It certainly helped me that day of riding 50 miles on a unicycle, and helps me other days as well.

I wrote a poem about my father:

SPIRIT

Away from here you flew
Long ago before I ever
Got my wings

Though a child when you left this world
In mind's vision
Your spirit remained

To build confidence was your way
always lighting life's darker corners
Even after death

Pushing will to the end of endurance
And like you before me, I am tested
Feeling your spirit, I prevail

Because your life's echo
Whispered
Refuse to fail

Refuse to fail. Humor helps us do that.

Chapter Nine
Pay Attention

What prompts your negative thoughts? Do you watch too much negative news or read the paper and focus on the stories of gloom and doom? Do you start to worry and become afraid?

With these humor habits, you can reduce your worry and fear. Less stress means better health and more happiness.

It simply requires that you pay attention.

Have you ever looked at newspaper headlines and tried to see how funny they can be by reframing the meaning? Here are some common examples:

- Police Begin Campaign To Run Down Jaywalkers
- Farmer Bill Dies In House
- Is There A Ring Of Debris Around Uranus?
- Prostitutes Appeal To Pope
- Panda Mating Fails: Veterinarian Takes Over
- Enraged Cow Injures Farmer with Ax

- War Dims Hope For Peace
- If Strike Isn't Settled Quickly, It May Last a While
- Red Tape Holds Up New Bridge
- Man Struck By Lightning Faces Battery Charge
- New Study Of Obesity Looks For Larger Test Group
- Steals Clock, Faces Time
- Queen Mary Having Bottom Scraped

If you look for these types of slips of the tongue, unintentionally suggestive and grammatical errors, you're bound to find some funny headlines once in a while.

What would happen if you skipped your negative thought provoking habits a few times a day? How many more positive thoughts would you have because of this minor change? Do you experience any repetitive thoughts that occur over and over? Do you experience any repetitive thoughts that occur over and over? Do you experience any repetitive thoughts that occur over and over?

What gives you positive thoughts? Comedy Central? A nice song? A book by your favorite comedian? Surfing funny YouTube videos? Old Willie who lives down the street that always has something outrageous to say?

The best way to influence your negative thoughts is to become more aware of what initiates them as well as what initiates your positive thoughts.

Use the hammer of humorous habits to beat negative thoughts into submission.

You can put a new twist on your old thoughts. A simple reframe often does the trick.

Say you applied for a promotion at work and didn't get it. You could go into an old way of "All-or-Nothing Thinking." Since you didn't get the job, you get depressed and feel worthless. (*Either I'm the best in the world or the worst in the world, all or nothing.*)

Instead, with your healthy humor habits, you could imagine all kinds of reasons for not getting the promotion. Perhaps this happened because of something you don't know yet, such as getting a new job that you end up loving!

We often put a giant spotlight on one negative occurrence: "I didn't get the promotion. I am a loser." or "Waking up late will ruin my entire day." With your humor spirit, you will see that is not the case at all.

(How come we never spotlight one good thing that happens and think, "Wow, my whole day will be amazing because I woke up early!"?)

Attitude is everything. Our thoughts can control our destiny, our lives. We can make ourselves happier, healthier by being more humorous.

The Cat's Diary

Day 983 of my captivity.

My captors continue to taunt me with bizarre little dangling objects.

They dine lavishly on fresh meat, while the other inmates and I are fed hash or some sort of dry nuggets. Although I make my contempt for the rations perfectly clear, nevertheless I must eat something to keep up my strength.

The only thing that keeps me going is my dream of escape. In an attempt to disgust them, I once again vomited on the carpet.

Today I decapitated a mouse and dropped its headless body at their feet. I had hoped this would strike fear into their hearts, since it clearly demonstrates my capabilities. However, they merely made condescending comments about what a "good little hunter" I am.

The Dog's Diary

8:00 am - Dog food! My favorite thing!

9:30am - A car ride! My favorite thing!

9:40am - A walk in the park! My favorite thing!

10:30am - Got rubbed and petted! My favorite thing!

12:00pm - Milk bones! My favorite thing!

1:00pm - Played in the yard! My favorite thing!

3:00pm - Wagged my tail! My favorite thing!

5:00pm - Dinner! My favorite thing!

7:00pm - Got to play ball! My favorite thing!

8:00pm - Wow! Watched TV with people! My favorite thing!

11:00pm - Sleeping on the bed! My favorite thing!

Do you know the folktale about the two travelers and the farmer? The first traveler came upon an old farmer. Eager to rest his feet, the wanderer hailed the countryman, who seemed happy enough to straighten his back and talk for a moment.

"What sort of people live in the next town?" asked the stranger.

"What were the people like were you've come from?" replied the farmer.

"They were a bad lot. Trouble makers all, and lazy too. The most selfish people in the world, and not one of them to be trusted."

"Is that so?" replied the farmer. "Well, I'm afraid you'll find the same sort in the next town."

Disappointed the traveler trudged on his way, and the farmer returned to his work.

Sometime later another stranger, coming from the same direction, hailed the farmer, and they stopped to talk. "What sort of people live in the next town?" he asked.

"What were the people like were you've come from?" replied the farmer once again.

"They were the best people in the world. Hardworking, honest and friendly. I'm sorry to be leaving them."

"Fear not" said the farmer. "You'll find the same sort in the next town."

What are you looking for? That is what you will find.

Professional comedians are constantly looking for new material through their everyday interactions. Do you try to see the humor in all your daily doings?

If you seek out humor, it will find you.

In Star Wars, Obi-Wan Kenobi (Ben) said: "The Force is what gives a Jedi his power. It's an energy field created by all living things. It surrounds us and penetrates us. It binds the galaxy together."

A basic premise was that the Force could be tapped into by Jedi Knights, evil Siths and just about anyone else in tune with it. There is also a Humor Force.

Obi Wan Ka-David: "The humor spirit force is an energy field created by all humorous things and things perceived to be humorous. It surrounds us. It binds us with others so we see our connections. It can sometimes make people laugh, but it can also give someone an inner smile, a feel-good sensation that was inspired by another human being, creature, event, place, movie, book, etc."

I have tested this belief many times and have found that the humor spirit force can be used to lighten someone's mood when they are anxious, angry, depressed, bored or just in a negative space.

As a Star Wars fan, I have imagined myself part of that world. Let me set the scene.

Obiwan ka-David and Darth David; an internal conversation about the first laugh between my mother and I after my return home (the phone ringing incident) and beginning to walk my first steps again.

Darth David: "Your life is over. (Heavy breathing sound) If you were dead, you would not have to live in extreme pain every day." (Heavy breathing sound)

Obi-wan kA-David: "Oh kiss my twenty-two-year old arthritic behind. You don't know what you're talking about. I had fun today. I saw my mother laugh for the first time since I came home in this crippled body. I laughed for the first time since I got home."

Darth David: (heavy breathing sound) "Yeah, well you'll never run again, never compete in an athletic event again. Never have a pain-free body again. Never -"

Obi-wan ka-David (interrupting Darth David): "Humor changed my life today. I'm not going back to YOU. Your days are over and you're just trying to pull me down. It won't work. Go away."

Darth David: "Oh, okay, (heavy breathing sound), but if you ever want to be depressed again, just let me know. Bye!"

Obi-wan ka-David: "Bye!"

For many years, I have attended an annual event called the "Mad Men on the Mountain" It's going on its 40th year. Just about all the "mad men" are very humorous. A bunch of baby boomers go up to mountains into a rugged, remote, wilderness areas for a weekend of laughter every year in early October. From the time we arrive to the time we leave, we laugh. We're from every and any occupation, many of us are psychotherapists, nurses and nurse practitioners, legal professions, psychologists, psychiatrists, other mental health professionals and administrators and some artsy people. There's other activities besides laughing but laughing is included in these as well. Activities such as Frisbee golf, a nice fire, and no women. One of the mad men wrote a song about this unique annual tradition.

We run, and we scream, and we party all night
Our problems are gone, they're all clean out of sight
Just one week a year, couple nights on our own
We kick out the jams, we drink and we smoke

We howl at the moon, and we dig in the dirt
We don't have to match our pants with our shirt
There's no shavin here, no showers to be had
If you can't stand the smell, that's just too damn bad

We're the Madmen on the mountain
We come out once a year and in the woods we stay
We're the Madmen on the mountain
We come out once a year, it keeps the wife and kids at bay

We're the Madmen runnin free
Camping in the woods in a big white teepee
We're the Madmen runnin wild
We may be getting older but we still ain't meek or mild

25 years and the legend still lives
No man takes more than he can give
We throw the disc closest to the pin
These guys are too good I'll never win

Beautiful mountain beautiful sky
We couldn't make it better even if we tried
I'll be back next year I can hardly wait
Cause I'm here right now and I'm feeling great

Never before had this ever occurred
Have we been compromised do we dare say a word
As she walked toward the fire they began to stir
And slowly a rumble arose from the herd

Hey what the hell they began to shout
She can't be here some said kick her out
But she'd reached out her hand to one of us in need
When he could no longer count on his trusted steed

So we gave her a break let her live in peace
Didn't push her in the fire didn't tie her to a tree
Do we change the rules let them all join in
Hell no are you crazy we are still madmen

Were the madmen on the mountain
We come out once a year and in the woods we stay
Were the madmen on the mountain
We do it once a year it keeps the wife and kids at bay

We got a new old madman blazing the path
Took over the reins from his dear old dad
We're all on board for this mountain fest
Don't see why this year can't be the best

Gotta hold on tight to what we all hold dear
Fires and rookies and whiskey and beer
Snake oil too if you are still so inclined
Never learned your lesson well maybe this time

As we move down the road the path is clear
Drink more whiskey, smoke and drink more beer
Sober up by Sunday and head on home
Another Madman in the books it's good as gold

Were the madmen on the mountain
We come out once a year and in the woods we stay
Were the madmen on the mountain
We do it once a year it keeps the wife and kids at bay

© Lyrics and Music by Ron Jorgensen

If you read the song close, you may notice one verse about the year my car broke down and I got stranded. I took the wrong turn and ended up on a dirt road 10 miles into the middle of nowhere. Now it was 11pm, nothing but acres and acres of ranch land. Instead of panicking, I smiled knowing a new story in my life's chapter was about to be created. I hopped on my unicycle with my backpack and sleeping bag attached to my back and a flashlight in my hand. I headed back towards the main road 10 miles away, though you couldn't call it much of a main road. Three miles into the pitch-black night I saw what looked like headlights in the distance. They got closer and closer and then the truck was upon me. I waved my arms and it actually stopped. I mean, who wouldn't stop for a unicyclist at midnight in the middle of a desolate road? Inside was a woman who stopped and asked what was going on? I explained I was on my way to Garner Canyon when my car broke down. She said that's where she was going and said let me hop in. Those there were used to me arriving quite late at night. As we approached the campsite, we were greeted by three full moons and though they looked pretty old, they weren't in the sky.

The point of this whole thing is that the laughter we share during these weekends sustain us until the following year. But I don't only have laughter once a year. It is a daily occurrence.

Think about your friends. Why are you friends with them? Hopefully your answer is because you enjoy being together and laughing together. Often, you're friends partly because you find the same things funny. I met my best friend, David Lempert, when I was 3 ½ and he was 4 years old. He lived across the street, that forbidden barrier that one could not cross without a grown-up.

There he was on the other side of the street, looking at the dirt in his front yard. I was compelled by curiosity to see what he was doing and ran across the street. He was watching a worm. A "big girl," maybe 7-years-old, walked by us. I picked up the worm and waved it in her face and she ran away screaming. David and I squealed with laughter. A friendship was born. Over fifty-six years later, we still laugh together and still pick up worms and put them in people's faces.

A great foundation of our friendship is humor. Humor is the foundation of many friendships, as it should be. If you do not have friends you laugh with, find some right away.

It can be easier than you think. When you treat humor as a necessity, use self-effacing humor, look for the funny, use humor to influence and improve communication, humorize your situations, act as if you are already humorous, and master your thoughts, improved relationships are right around the corner.

When you put these habits into practice, your life can change.

I was overtaken by the spirit of humor during a serious lecture in a Yeshiva in Jerusalem. A Yeshiva is an institution for Torah study and the study of Talmud primarily within Orthodox Judaism attended by males. I was sitting with a friend across from me and the Rabbi said something that wasn't particularly funny. What was funny was the look on my friend's face of total confusion and not understanding a word the rabbi was talking about. I started laughing and then so did he.

We laughed hard enough that we had to bury our heads in our arms on the table. The fatal mistake we made, which gave the Humor Spirit total control of us, was that as we were regaining control, we both peeked up at each other at the same time. Seeing his eyebrow and one eye appear above his buried face beneath his arm and elbow was too much and I started cracking up, much louder than him. Then he became even louder when he looked under the table where I pointed, and he noticed that I had totally pissed my pants. We had to get up and leave the room.

As I left, still laughing quite loudly, my soaked pants were revealed to all and the spirit of humor spread throughout the room. Fortunately, the Rabbi also had a sense of humor and ended the lecture early, also laughing and explaining that sometimes we come closer to the almighty through laugher "as David apparently has done today." I believe the almighty was pleased, because as I left the building, a heavy rain began, blessing and soaking me and hiding the evidence of my laughter torn bladder so it would not be revealed to the public at large.

I am eternally grateful for the spirit of humor.

Chapter 10
The Spirit of Humor

The spirit of humor includes jokes, play, laughter, wit, sarcasm, exaggeration, surprise, etc. and the list goes on and on. We have acquired our humor knowledge through our senses, culture and personal experiences. Additionally, there are invisible and "unknowable" aspects of humor that play a part in humorgy.

Some elements are on a subconscious level, for example, your humor spirit's nature. Let's say you're reading this sentence and suddenly, you remember the funniest thing that ever happened in your life. The force of humor overtakes you and you smile and feel warm. You do not feel warm because you just wet your pants, but because there is something unknowable involved and as such, unexplainable. The part of humor that is unexplainable in words, but present and felt during laughter, play, etc. is the spirit of humor.

There is a Humor Spirit Aura. Okay this can get a little weird, but stay with me. You might wish to consider the possibility that the Humor Spirit Aura could be an integral part of your personal space. When two people invade each other's personal space, they sometimes laugh nervously out of feeling uncomfortable. There is more to the story than that. You are unconsciously projecting your humorgy, as are they.

When these forces combine, they create a sense of happiness. If this was just "nervousness," there would be high anxiety and stress and negative feelings. Happiness is not conducive with these negative feelings; therefore, the humor spirits' presence may be another explanation for this reaction.

Humor Spirit Theory states that humor is a good and healthy feeling that comes from a positive place. You KNOW it when you feel it. Definitions that rely on validity and reliability, scientifically researched and anally correct hypotheses may be important, but that importance fades in the light of feeling and experiencing the true spirit of humor. There are emotional, cognitive, physical and spiritual aspects of humor, but suffice it to say that when you are a humorous person, you recognize and know humor when its spirit is upon you.

You also have the ability to create or induce the humor spirit's presence. Most of the time we can "control" this spirit, but we have all probably experienced a time when the spirit of humor overtook us and we laughed uncontrollably and no matter how hard we tried, we couldn't stop. Boy, what a great feeling that is!

There were some great TV scenes that depicted this, like the Mary Tyler Moore show episode titled: "Chuckles Bites the Dust." WJM-TV's children's show host, Chuckles the Clown, dressed as a peanut, is accidentally killed by an elephant, and his death provokes numerous newsroom jokes by Murray, Lou, and Ted--who are berated for their insensitivity by a shocked Mary.

They all attend the funeral, and once it starts, Mary cannot hold back the giggles that well up until she is laughing uncontrollably. It is an incredible example of the Spirit of Humor in action and supremely funny as well. Another scene of uncontrollable laughter was when Steve Allen was live on his show and did a news piece and just began to laugh uncontrollably and couldn't stop. Since it was live, all they could do was film him laughing for over five minutes.

There are dozens of great moments of uncontrolled laughter on TV and in movies and in life. I'm sure you have your own. If you don't, now is the time to begin searching for them.

Another example dates to 1995 in Hyde Park, New York when President Bill Clinton laughed uncontrollably at a joke made by Russian President Boris Yeltsin at a summit at FDR's home. The event was photographed by Allan Tannenbaum. This probably did more for international diplomacy and peace than one hundred hours bickering over a negotiation table or trying to instill fear in the ones on the other side of the table.

Benjamin Franklin won the heart of France with his quick wit and wonderful sense of humor. I suggest that all diplomats be required to take a course in improving their sense of humor. The worldview of the U.S. or "us" would probably change dramatically for the better.

The Spirit of Humor is a power we revere.

I remember wondering why did I have to get arthritis. Why me? I wanted to ask g-d why and he answered me in a dream that night. A giant man with a long white beard sitting on a white concrete throne floating in a cloud above my bed said, "Okay, I'll let you ask me that one question, but I'll never answer you again so make sure this is the question you want to ask me."

I said, "Okay. Why did I get arthritis?"

He answered, "There's something about you that just pissed me off."

(Full disclosure: This quip is adapted from Stephen King who made the joke, "When his life was ruined, his family killed, his farm destroyed, Job knelt down on the ground and yelled up to the heavens, "Why god? Why me?" and the thundering voice of God answered, "There's just something about you that pisses me off.")

The spirit of humor has kept me healthy as possible and I am absolutely happy. I implement humor in everything. When I die, my final words will be, "Tell them I said something funny."

I hope you see this book as a gift. (One that you don't eat. Let the hamsters do that.) We buy things for people all the time to give as gifts. This book is one such thing. A greater gift that you can give others every day of your life is the gift of humor.

That reminds me of the famous Chinese proverb: "Give a man a fish and you'll feed him for a day. Teach a man to fish, and you'll feed him for a lifetime." I would add, "Give him a grill and he'll enjoy all that fish a lot more, unless it is anchovies." I hate anchovies.

This book is about the fabric of humor. Think of humor like a quilt. Just like a quilt represents the many racial, national, religious, and cultural groups that live in our Western civilization, so does the type of humor you use reflect your personal tastes, background and your socioeconomic, religious, pseudo-scientific New Age perspectives. I hope you have enjoyed the tapestry of humor woven throughout this book. And I hope you like quilt analogies.

Let your laughs ring forth. Embrace the concepts in this book with your whole being.

If we laugh only from our mouths and add nothing from our hearts, then your laughter is lacking the spirit of humor. After we have had a good laugh, as beautiful as it can be, there may linger in our hearts some precious sentiments of joy emoted from the laughter, which we are unable to express outwardly. This is the laughter that comes from the joy of our most intimate feeling and thoughts. And yet, we may not be able to find the words for this expression.

Thoughts that lie too deep for words may be expressed by our silent smile. Some of our deepest joys never find expression in words, they remain in the realm of our humor spirit.

The poet John Keats wrote: "Heard melodies are sweet, but those unheard are sweeter." From time to time we have heard melodies which play not upon the ear but within our humor spirit, melodies which originate not outside ourselves but in the inner most part of ourselves. I have seen smiles on faces that have revealed these inner most melodies, music from the spirit of humor.

Music from our humor spirit emerges out of our inner depths – created by our fears and our hopes, by our guilt and our gratitude, by our needs and by our aspirations. The cathartic release of these inner melodies gives rise to a level of awareness of spiritual connections that goes beyond the limited understanding of the mind.

Could you ever put into words the feeling of collapsing into uncontrollable laughter and feeling it blanket you with its occurrence? You could not, but you could smile and nod to another who has experienced the same thing.

Allow in the spirit of humor. It's a beautiful thing.

The Chapter That's Not a Chapter

Due to my sense of humor, I have received many rewards. Seriously. I have received first class upgrades, free tickets to shows, free wine and the list goes on and on. These are the type of things that happen to people that read this book. Disclaimer: this is not a promise and actual results will vary for many reasons including reading conditions, level of comprehension, and sense of humor you're starting out with before reading this book. For instance, if you are like a baby tree, your sense of humor can grow for years just like the tree, but if you are more like a tree stump, it's very difficult to grow. Become the tree and this book will nourish you with humor like water for trees. Humor skills are real and can be developed by anyone. And make you richer.

People define riches in various ways. If I'm with another person and that person is suffering in some way, I consider myself richer if I can alleviate some of that suffering, especially while writing run-on sentences at the same time. You too can be richer for the experience (and sharing your sense of humor and run-on sentences). A person is beautiful if they can share a rich sense of humor and love for their fellow beings.

The following creed is based on the Creed of a US Marine: My Rifle. I changed the focus from rifle to humor.

My Sense of Humor: The Creed of a Humorous Person.

This is my sense of humor. There are many like it, but this one is mine. My sense of humor is my best friend. It is my life. I must master it as I must master my life.

My sense of humor, without me, is useless. Without my sense of humor, I am useless. I must laugh because of my sense of humor. I must laugh harder than others who may try to make fun of me.

My sense of humor and myself know that what counts in this life is not the negative thoughts we think, but our ability to use humor to change them to positive. We know that it is the laughs that count. We will laugh...

My sense of humor is connected to my spirit, even as I, because it is a critical part of my life. Thus, I will learn to use my sense of humor in times of trouble. I will learn its weaknesses, its strength, and its type. I will always use it against the ravages of life. I will keep my sense of humor clean and healthy. Apollo has his Creed, and this is my creed.

David's Laws

First Law: Things are usually easier than they look and if it turns out they're not, it's because there is a new lesson to learn that will save your ass down the road later.

Second Law: Things don't take as long as you would think they do. If they end up taking longer, it's because you were going to have a fatal accident if the "thing" finished sooner.

Third Law: In any field of endeavor, anything that can go wrong probably won't, but if it does, it's because you'll end up better off that it did. (See Second Law.)

Fourth Law: If there is a possibility that several things can go wrong, then the one that will cause the least damage will be the one to go wrong.

Fifth Law: If you perceive that there are four possible solutions to a problem, but don't like any of them, then a fifth solution will promptly develop.

Sixth Law: Left to themselves, things tend to find their own resolutions, that is unless they are human.

Seventh Law: You get to make up your own laws.

½ Law: Always have fun.

Backward

Most books have a Foreword, but this book has a Backward as well. I thought that you, the reader of 7 ½ Habits, have a great sense of humor or are in the process of developing one, therefore you deserve to have both a Foreword and a Backward, not to mention a Fast Foreword and the value-added Postface, all for the same "average priced book."

No additional charges were incurred for these added values and no animals were harmed by adding these additions either. Although one of our hamsters died during the writing of this edition. A thorough investigation concluded that the hamster's death was not related to the writing of the book and in fact it may have prolonged Mr. Walk'ums life. I would read new material to Mr. Walk'ums and he really loved this book. I know it's true because I gave him the proof copy and he ate it in a matter of days.

Even though he died, the interesting thing is that this hamster who ate a book lived longer than any other hamster we've ever had. Mr. Walk'ums also had a much better sense of humor. This hamster danced, had acrobatic abilities, didn't bite, and if you sat him on a tiny dollhouse size toilet, he would poop in it. That's how smart Mr. Walk'ums was.

Hey, wait a minute. I just discovered that we had a gerbil not a hamster, according to my wife. Laurie said we switched from hamsters to gerbils because they are cheaper and don't run around on wheels all night. I apologize to any hamster owners out there for the misinformation. And to Mr. Walk'ums.

So now you know a Backward is like a Foreword but spelled with "back" instead of "fore." Both have the word "word" in common and that is an important word. Without words you wouldn't be reading this book, and without reading this book you would have been doing something else, like walking around your house and possibly tripping and breaking your neck, so you can actually say, this book may have saved your life.
You're welcome.

Appendix B: Formerly Appendix A

Resources and recommendations for further information. This section was written to replace the "Appendix A" which had to be removed due to emergency surgery. The "Gallbladder" section also had to go.

The following people have influenced the writing of this book. If you get a chance to hear them speak, or read anything thing they've written, it's highly recommended.

Steve Allen, Don Baird, Lee Berk, Karyn Buxman, Lenny Dave Chip Lutz, Ed Dunkelblau, Allen Klein, Paul McGhee, Rod Martin C.W. Metcalf , Mary Kay Morrison, Lenny Ravich, Yakov Smirnoff, Steve Sultanoff and Patty Wooten.

Here's a link to the Cut website article that features the humor style quiz: https://www.thecut.com/article/whats-your-humor-style.html

A few more links, but no Princess Zelda:

Humor Styles, Self-Esteem and Subjective Happiness
http://ssweb.cityu.edu.hk/download/RS/E-Journal/journal2.pdf
A great study that investigates the positive and negative humor styles described by Rod Martin and mentioned in the quiz above.

Short Alleles, Bigger Smiles? The Effect of 5-HTTLPR on Positive Emotional Expressions.
https://www.ncbi.nlm.nih.gov/pmc/articles/PMC4861141/

Who Benefits From Humor-Based Positive Psychology Interventions? The Moderating Effects of Personality Traits and Sense of Humor.
https://www.ncbi.nlm.nih.gov/pmc/articles/PMC5985328/

The Association for Applied and Therapeutic Humor
https://www.aath.org/

The Jacobson Joy Inventory: A New Look at Measuring Depression
https://www.amazon.com/Jacobson-Joy-Inventory-Measuring-Depression/dp/0692839534

Some more recommendations, because I had my picture taken with them…

McGhee, P. (1996) Health, Healing and the Amuse System.

Fry WF Jr, Salameh WA, editors. (1987) Handbook of Humor and Psychotherapy: Advances in the Clinical Use of Humor. Sarasota, Fla,

Litt, D. (2017) Thanks, Obama: My Hopey, Changey White House Years

Yakov Live on Broadway (1994) As Long As We Both Shall Laugh!

Pollak, K. How I Slept My Way to the Middle: Secrets and Stories from Stage, Screen, and Interwebs (2012)

Shira, Laurie, Joshua, Yosef and Samuel Jacobson 2004

Laurie, David, Yosef, Joshua, Shira and Samuel Jacobson
Ten years later, but still some time ago

From my family to your family, thank you for taking the time to read this book and if you enjoyed the read, please consider letting me know by leaving a review on Amazon. I hope you continue to become more Humorous, Happier and Healthier!

Made in the USA
San Bernardino, CA
12 September 2019